In Context

Functional Skills English

ENTRY 3 – LEVEL 2

Construction Workbook

John Meed
Anna Rossetti

Nelson Thornes

This edition published in 2013 by:
Nelson Thornes Ltd
Delta Place
27 Bath Road
CHELTENHAM
GL53 7TH
United Kingdom

13 14 15 16 17 / 10 9 8 7 6 5 4 3 2 1

A catalogue record for this book is available from the British Library

ISBN 978 1 4085 1830 4

Cover image: Kudryashka/Shutterstock

Illustrations by James Elston and Paul McCaffrey, Sylvie Poggio Agency

Page make-up by Pantek Media, Maidstone

Printed in Turkey by Ömür Printing and Binding Company

Acknowledgements
The authors and the publisher would like to thank the following for permission to reproduce material:

Text
p7, Dermatitis information sourced from Health and Safety Executive © Crown Copyright 2012; p9, 'A Woman's Place? Sure Group Apprentice wins Women in Construction Award 2012', Sure Group website; p11, quotation from Anne McVicker the Chief Executive of Women's Tec, and Joanne Fuller, Construction Manager with Morgan Ashurst (http://www.cskills.org); p11, quotation from Tessa Jowell the Olympics Minister (www.london2012.com); p15, 'Top 10 eco-buildings' by Vikki Miller, Copyright Guardian News & Media Ltd 2007; p19, 'Think pink if you want to deter building-site thieves' by Lucy Tobin, Copyright Guardian News & Media Ltd 2011; pp22, security fencing information (http://www.safesitefacilities.co.uk/security-fencing); p29, 'Keeping Safe on roofs', sourced from Health and Safety Executive © Crown Copyright 2012; p31, Gwyndaf Davies re-roofing in Carmarthenshire, Health and Safety Executive © Crown Copyright 2012; p35, 'No more waste: Building a health and social care centre', adapted from www.wrap.org.uk, © WRAP 2012; p39, 'Sleaford Construction company lands £9.5m energy plant contract', © Lincolnshire Echo 2012; p57, Heating Equipment Testing and Approval Scheme information, © Copyright 2012 HETAS. All Rights Reserved (http://www.hetas.co.uk); p59, 'Health and safety for smaller builders', Health and Safety Executive © Crown Copyright 2012; p61, Hide and seek accident, © Copyright RoSPA (http://www.rospa.com); p69, 'Smooth operators', Duncan Styles (www.diy-power-tools.co.uk); pp71 and 72, Axminster AWDS12H 300mm Disc Sander and Axminster DS12DL 300mm Disc Sander Copyright © Axminster Power Tool Centre Ltd 2012, adapted from http://www.axminster.co.uk; p79, 'Building London 2012', Copyright © Olympic Delivery Authority; p81, 'Olympic velodrome on list for building of the year prize', Copyright Guardian News & Media Ltd 2011; p85, 'A rotten business', 2012 Copyright Safeguard Europe Ltd (www.safeguardeurope.com); p95, 'Working abroad', © Copyright 2012 Graduate Prospects Ltd (http://www.prospects.ac.uk); p95, 'Working abroad – The CSCS card', adapted from www.cscs.uk.com; p99, 'Employment rights of young workers', GOV.UK © Crown Copyright 2012 (www.direct.gov.uk); p105, 'Revealed: Shoddy work of jailed cowboy builder caught in TV sting after £370,000 fraud', © Copyright Daily Mail 2012; p108, 'Tighter checks to keep cowboy builders out', Department for Communities and Local Government © Crown Copyright 2012; p109, 'Green-belt land and its purpose', sourced from http://politics-greenbelt.org.uk; p111, 'Hotel ordered to remove unauthorised outdoor drinking area', © Copyright Brighouse Echo 2012; p115, 'Working for yourself – Being self-employed', information sourced from the Citizens Advice Bureau: Advice guide (http://www.adviceguide.org.uk); p117, 'Employment Status', sourced from www.taxchampion.co.uk; p119, 'Built to last', text written from information deriving from www.rafupwood.co.uk and www.bovishomes.co.uk; p121, 'Buying a new home', information sourced from www.taylorwimpey.co.uk; p121, 'Buying for the first time', information sourced from www.bovishomes.co.uk.

Images
Alamy: p22 (© Justin Kase z03z), p28 (© Aurora Photos), p35 (© Justin Kase z11z), p45 (© Adam G. Gregor), p55 (© www.maximimages.com), p59 (© Paul Broadbent), p79 (© Edd Westmacott), p81 (© Anthony Collins Cycling), p14 (© Adrian Sherratt); iStockphoto: p89 (SteveDF); Shutterstock: p29 (Vladislav Gajic), p49 (Andreas G. Karelias), p65 (auremar), p69 (vidguten), p84 (auremar), p94 (Kamira), p109 (Steve Heap), p119 (RTImages); p7 ('Contains public sector information published by the Health and Safety Executive and licensed under the Open Government Licence v1.0'); p9 (courtesy of Suregroup); p13 (ZEDfactory); p13 (Flagship); p13 (Courtesy of Kingsmead Primary School); pp71–72 (courtesy Axminster Tool Centre); p85 (Safeguard Europe Ltd).

Every effort has been made to trace the copyright holders but if any have been inadvertently overlooked the publisher will be pleased to make the necessary arrangements at the first opportunity.

Contents

Introduction

"Functional skills are the fundamental, applied skills in English, mathematics, and information and communication technology (ICT) which help people to gain the most from life, learning and work."

Ofqual (2012), Criteria for Functional Skills Qualifications

This workbook is designed to present functional English in a variety of contexts to make it accessible and relevant to you, as Construction candidates. It is intended to be written in, so use it as a record of your progress!

Being 'functional' means that you will:

- be able to apply skills to all sorts of real-life contexts
- have the mental ability to take on challenges in a range of new settings
- be able to work independently
- realise that tasks often need persistence, thought and reflection.

Features of this workbook are:

 **Source**

These pages will cover important aspects of Construction and consist of some interesting source materials, such as newspaper articles or industry-related information, followed by various questions and activities for you to complete.

 FOCUS ON

Each Focus on is typically 2 pages long and will teach you specific Functional Skills. They include:

- guidance on the skill
- one or more activities to practise the skill.

Good luck!

Worker suffers dermatitis after spraying paint

Isocyanate is a hazardous substance which is widely used in paints. A Health and Safety Executive (HSE) inspector said: 'Isocyanate is subject to workplace exposure limits because of its ability to damage workers' health.' Employers are required by law to ensure that those at risk of exposure are protected. If they fail to do this, the HSE may prosecute them for breaching the Control of Substances Hazardous to Health Regulations 2002 (COSHH).

Exposure to isocyanate can cause long-term and sometimes life-threatening illness. It is the second-largest cause of occupational asthma, and can also cause conjunctivitis, dermatitis, bronchitis and rhinitis. Spray mist containing isocyanate may cause or worsen existing asthma. Once people are affected even very low exposure levels can trigger an attack.

Case study

A worker was repainting a gas pipeline. He was driving an open-cabbed vehicle with a sprayer attached. The paint contained isocyanate. Afterwards the skin around his face and hands started to feel sore and he was diagnosed with dermatitis. The open cab meant that he was exposed to the paint as it was being sprayed and he was likely to have been exposed to up to 10 times the workplace limit for the chemical.

His employer should have reduced the risk by providing him with proper protective equipment, such as breathing apparatus, overalls, face mask, etc. Also, even though the type of work meant that there was no alternative to the type of paint that could be used, it could have been applied with a brush, instead of by a spraygun, which would have reduced the risk of exposing him to isocyanate.

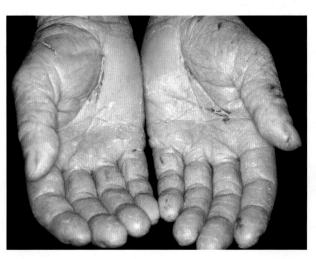

A Read the text and answer these questions.

1 How did exposure to isocyanate affect the worker?

2 What was the worker doing when he was exposed to the chemical?

3 Who prosecuted a company for breaking health and safety law?

4 What two things meant the worker was exposed to the chemical?

5 Which regulations?

6 Why does isocyanate have a workplace exposure limit?

7 How could the risk have been avoided?

B In a group, discuss these questions. You could make notes below.

1 Do you think it is important to be able to prosecute employers who do not protect the safety of workers? Why?

2 What might happen if there were no legal controls?

C Look up the meaning of the following words. Choose two of the words and write each of them in separate sentences.

exposure   occupational   dermatitis   contaminate   alternative

1

2

D Fill the gaps in these sentences using the following words:

brush   asthma   prosecute   protective   open-cabbed

1 Isocyanate is the second-largest cause of occupational [   ].

2 An [   ] vehicle increases the risk of exposure.

3 The HSE can [   ] companies that do not protect workers from hazardous chemicals.

4 The paint could have been applied with a [   ] instead of a spray gun.

5 The company did not provide the worker with proper [   ] equipment.

E Read through this text and answer the questions that follow on page 8.

Dermatitis is a skin condition caused by contact with something that irritates the skin or causes an allergic reaction. It usually occurs where the irritant touches the skin.

Symptoms can include redness, blistering, flaking, weeping, cracking or swelling.

Someone who has dermatitis may experience symptoms of itching and pain. The signs and symptoms of this condition can be so bad that the sufferer is unable to carry on working.

Dermatitis can occur quickly after contact with a strong irritant, or over a longer period from repeated contact with weaker irritants. If someone develops an allergy, this may become permanent so that any future contact with the substance may cause an allergic reaction.

In building work, dermatitis can be caused by many things including wet cement, solvents, dusts, oils, greases and cleaning agents.

1 Complete this sentence.

Dermatitis is a skin condition caused by contact with something that

2 Give three symptoms of dermatitis.

3 Give three substances that may cause dermatitis in building work.

F Write four sentences about the risks to skin that occur in building work, and what you can do to protect your skin.

1

2

3

4

Sure Group Apprentice wins Women in Construction Award 2012

Sure Group staff are celebrating today after Caroline Rhodes was awarded 'Best Apprentice/New Starter 25 and Over' at a sparkling black-tie dinner held in Manchester on Wednesday evening. Caroline was shortlisted from over 80 nominations, along with fellow Sure Group apprentice Danielle Pendlebury, who was nominated for 'Best Apprentice/New Starter under 25'.

The Women in Construction Awards, now in its sixth year, provides a showcase for the brightest and the best female achievers in the house-building and wider construction industries.

Caroline was a worthy winner. After 13 years in local government, Caroline followed her dream to become a heating engineer. A single mum, she self-funded her studies, while still working. She was overjoyed with her award and said, 'It is amazing to be recognised for the job that I love to do. Being a gas engineer is brilliant – I have trained hard, and feel that I am making a valuable contribution to keeping people safe in their homes.'

Caroline is part of Sure Group's Halton Housing Trust Team. Colin Knox, Gas Safety and Asset Administrator for Halton Housing Trust (HHT) said, 'We are all delighted for Caroline. She is a tremendous addition to Sure Group and HHT. Her enthusiasm, positive attitude, "can do" approach and technical ability have been a real pleasure to see.'

It was also a very proud evening for Danielle, her family and all of the Sure Group Team. From an early age Danielle went to work at weekends with her dad, Neil, a gas engineer also working at Sure Group. She has successfully completed an NVQ Level 3 and an Advanced Apprenticeship Framework. She volunteers for additional unpaid work in the evenings and at weekends with other engineers to hone her diagnostic skills. She now specialises in diagnosing faults.

Darren Cunningham, Chief Executive of Sure Group, said, 'I am very proud of Danielle and Caroline, and all of the apprentices that we have within our business. At Sure Group our people are our greatest strength, and our heating engineers are the most visible aspect of our business, dealing face to face with customers every day. Apprenticeships help to drive our business forward, so we are keen to attract motivated and enthusiastic recruits like Caroline and Danielle, and provide them with a high standard of quality training and a career they can be proud of.'

Caroline and Danielle with Darren Cunningham

A Which of these statements are true and which are false?

1 This was the third year of the Women in Construction Awards.   True ☐   False ☐

2 Caroline spent 13 years in local government before becoming a heating engineer.   True ☐   False ☐

3 Caroline's father is a gas engineer at Sure Group.   True ☐   False ☐

4 Danielle specialises in diagnosing faults.   True ☐   False ☐

B Who's who?

Tick the boxes to show which statements are true for which person.

		Caroline	Danielle
1	Is aged over 25		
2	Is aged under 25		
3	Is a single mother		
4	Went to work with her dad each weekend		
5	Is a heating engineer		
6	Is an award winner		

C Who said what?

1	'I have trained hard, and feel that I am making a valuable contribution to keeping people safe in their homes.'	
2	'Her enthusiasm, positive attitude, "can do" approach and technical ability have been a real pleasure to see.'	
3	'Our heating engineers are the most visible aspect of our business, dealing face to face with customers every day.'	

D Work with a partner. Add capital letters and full stops to these sentences.

1 sure group staff are celebrating today after caroline rhodes won an award in manchester on wednesday evening

2 the women in construction awards is now in its sixth year

3 darren cunningham is chief executive of sure group

4 from an early age, danielle went to work at weekends with her dad, neil, a gas engineer also working at sure group

E Read these quotes.

'The construction industry remains a male-dominated environment. At present women account for only 10 per cent of the workforce, with the vast majority of those working in a clerical capacity.' Anne McVicker, Chief Executive of Women's Tec

'For me, the Women in Construction Conference helped to dispel the myth that the industry is a male bastion. I have come across many other women in my job who have various roles in the industry including painters and decorators, joiners, architects or engineers.' Joanne Fuller, Construction Manager with Morgan Ashurst

'The London 2012 Women into Construction project is an excellent example of how we are using the Olympic Games to blaze a trail for equal employment opportunities. Not only will this programme help more women get construction jobs working on the Games, but [it will] also make a significant contribution to breaking down gender barriers within the industry as a whole.' Tessa Jowell, Former Olympics Minister

In a group, discuss these questions.

- Anne McVicker says that construction remains 'a male-dominated environment' while Joanne Fuller says it is a 'myth that the industry is a male bastion'. Who do you agree with?

- What factors may put women off working in construction?

- Do you think things are changing?

- Are projects such as London 2012 Women into Construction a good idea?

F If someone said the following things to you about women in construction, what would you say?

- You cannot just reply 'I agree' or 'I disagree'.

- You need to add something more to the discussion.

1 'It's just too much hassle having special toilets and changing rooms.'
  What would you say?

2 'Companies need to make more of an effort to employ and train women.'
  What would you say?

3 'Women just do not want to work in construction.'
  What would you say?

G Write a short letter to the paper. Aim for three paragraphs about:

- how you heard about the Women in Construction awards
- what you think about the awards
- whether you think more should be done to encourage women into the industry.

(Your address)

(Date)

(The paper's address)

Dear

Yours sincerely/faithfully

(Your signature)

FOCUS ON **Proper nouns**

Sentences start with a capital letter, but capital letters are also used for proper nouns. Proper nouns are the names of a specific or unique:

• person

• place

• organisation

• item or brand.

Days of the week and months also have capitals (e.g. Monday, July), as do titles such as Mr, Mrs and Ms.

They are different from common nouns, which do not have capitals.

Here are some examples:

Common noun	Proper noun
person	Mr Paul Burstow
city	Sheffield
country	France
company	Bristol Tool Company
organisation	Chartered Institute of Building
drill	Black & Decker
place	Wembley Stadium

 A Four of these words are proper nouns. Which ones are they?

• Peter

• Son

• Builder

• Oxford

• Wickes

• Carillion

• Plumber

• Hammer

B The sentences below have no capital letters in them. Underline each word that should start with a capital letter.

1 mr james stevens is the manager of jim's plumbing.

2 julie is the bookkeeper and works on wednesday, thursday and friday.

3 the plumbers said they could do the job in july.

4 the construction industry council is based in london.

5 the green construction board promotes sustainable construction.

6 the midland metro is being extended in birmingham.

7 the decorator used trade paints from dulux.

8 the plasterer bought two trowels and a plastic float.

9 the health and safety executive enforces health and safety law.

10 marshalltown brick trowel blades are forged from a single piece of steel.

C Give an example of a proper noun for each category below.

1 Person

2 Equipment

3 Company

4 Brand

5 Town

6 Place

BowZed, Bow, east London

East London is perhaps not where you'd expect to find one of the country's most sustainable buildings, but the BowZed block of four, zero fossil-energy flats is so well insulated that there are no central heating systems in the flats. The residents get 40 per cent of their electricity from solar panels and 50 per cent from a micro wind turbine on the stair tower. Hot water comes from a boiler powered by wood pellets and the residents say three tonnes is enough to fuel the four flats for a year.

The show apartment cost 15 per cent more to buy than an average property of the same size, and was bought for £275,000. As a result, environmentalists claim that there is a good market for eco-housing.

Honingham earth-sheltered social housing scheme, Honingham, Norfolk

Gary and Keron Lawson live in one of four two-bedroom bungalows with running costs of just £3.80 per week. There's no conventional heating or cooling system and the development has zero carbon emissions. The houses are earth-sheltered, meaning the north, west and east walls are covered by an earth mound. Only the south face of the house is left open to capture heat and light from the sun.

'Light comes through the full-length windows and it stays at 22°C throughout the winter,' Gary says. 'We hadn't heard of anything like this at all before we moved in.'

Peddars Way housing association, who commissioned and manage the scheme, plan more earth-sheltered homes and an earth-sheltered business campus.

Kingsmead Primary School, Northwich, Cheshire

Kingsmead Primary School in Cheshire is designed to help pupils learn more about the environment. The active voltage displays show how much energy the solar panels produce. An electronic meter shows how much rainwater is collected by the inverted roof.

To stop the little ones nodding off during a long lesson, a system (run on renewable energy) automatically opens and shuts the windows, skylights and blinds. This allows fresh air to flow through the building. It also shades pupils where necessary.

A Write down what each of these words means.

1	Fossil energy	
2	Environmentalists	
3	Conventional	
4	Commissioned	
5	Inverted	
6	Renewable	

B Which building(s) have the following features?

1 Solar panels

2 Stays at 22 °C in winter

3 A wind turbine

4 Windows that open automatically

5 Covered by an earth mound

6 A roof designed to collect rain

C Choose the correct answer to each of these questions.

1 How much of their electricity do BowZed residents get from solar panels?

    a) 30 per cent ☐

    b) 40 per cent ☐

    c) 50 per cent ☐

    d) 60 per cent ☐

2 According to the text, Honingham running costs are:

a) £2.80 per week ☐

b) £3.18 per week ☐

c) £3.80 per week ☐

d) £38.00 per week ☐

D Describe two ways in which the design of Kingsmead Primary School helps pupils.

1

2

E Fill in the gaps in this paragraph using the following words:

money   wasted   business   heat   construction   transport   reduces

Eco-friendly [_____] means building in ways that benefit — or do not harm — the environment. Good planning means fewer things are [_____]. Using local materials reduces how much energy you need to [_____] them and benefits local businesses. Less energy goes into the manufacture and production of green products and this [_____] carbon emissions. Eco-friendly design also reduces how much energy is needed to [_____] the building. Many of these things also make good [_____] sense. For example, cutting back on waste saves [_____].

F With a partner, discuss eco-buildings.

• Have you heard of eco-buildings before?

• Do you know of any ways to make a building more eco-friendly?

• What more could be done to make buildings eco-friendly?

How well did you listen to each other while discussing eco-buildings?

Give yourselves a score for each statement:

- Score 3 if this was true most of the time.
- Score 2 if this was sometimes true.
- Score 1 if this did not happen very often.

	Statement	Score (3–1)
1	We took turns to speak.	
2	We listened carefully when the other person spoke.	
3	We looked at each other often while we were talking.	
4	We avoided interrupting each other.	
5	We showed when we agreed (e.g. by nodding, saying 'yes').	
6	We asked questions to check we had understood.	

H Note down two things you could do another time to make sure you listen to each other carefully.

1

2

 Think about two different ways to make buildings more eco-friendly. Write a paragraph about each.

Example 1:

Example 2:

Think pink if you want to deter building-site thieves

Not even Bob the Builder ever used a pink digger on his building site – but research at Birmingham City University suggests it could put off thieves.

Professors David Edwards and Gary Holt began their research project after spending years working in the building industry. Edwards started his career as a bricklayer, then worked his way up the ranks. Holt first worked as a construction manager in the building and civil engineering industries.

'Theft from building and civil engineering sites is common – by petty thieves, but also by organised gangs who use the money to fund people trafficking, prostitution, drugs and even terrorism,' says Edwards. 'Much stolen plant is broken down and sold as parts in this country and abroad.'

'Most machinery found on building sites has a high resale value, so it offers thieves fast, easy and high returns,' adds Holt. 'A 20 tonne excavator can cost up to £100,000, and yet stealing one is arguably easier than stealing a £5,000 second-hand family car.'

Edwards and Holt suggest that the cost of plant theft in the UK is between £1.1 million and £1.5 million a week. In 2006 they began working

closely with victims, machine manufacturers and anti-theft device manufacturers to look at how burglaries happen and how they might be prevented.

Their studies showed the best deterrents to be locking machines in awkward positions, for example with excavating arms extended; adding company logos and painting machinery pink.

'Painting a machine pink is not expensive, but can be a strong deterrent,' says Holt. 'Bright identifying colours put off a thief, and make it more difficult for them to sell stolen parts – they'd have to be resprayed first. Why steal a pink one when thousands of yellow machines already exist for the second-hand market?'

The academics admit the scheme could become a victim of its own success. 'If everyone started to "paint it pink", then pink machines would no longer look out of place,' Edwards concedes. 'The real message is to make the plant as conspicuous as possible and add company livery and logos to make the thief look elsewhere.'

A   Which of these statements are true and which are false?

1   Gary Holt worked as a construction manager.   True ☐   False ☐

2   A 20 tonne excavator can cost £5,000.   True ☐   False ☐

3   Plant theft costs £100,000 a week.   True ☐   False ☐

4   Adding company livery and logos can put off a thief. True ☐   False ☐

B   Write down answers to these questions.

1   What was David Edwards' first job?

[   ]

2   Where do Edwards and Holt work now?

[   ]

3   Who steals machinery from building sites?

[   ]

4   Where do thieves sell stolen machinery?

[   ]

5   Suggest two ways to put off a thief:

a) [   ]

b) [   ]

6   Why is it harder for a thief to sell parts from a pink machine?

C   Add ONE comma to each of these sentences.

1   David Edwards started his career as a bricklayer then he worked his way up the ranks.

2   Gangs who use the money to fund people trafficking prostitution and drugs.

3   You can put off thieves by locking machines in awkward positions adding company logos and painting machinery pink.

4   If everyone started to 'paint it pink' pink machines would no longer look out of place.

D For each of the following words, write a sentence that contains the word.

1 research

2 engineering

3 awkward

4 deterrent

5 conspicuous

E In your group discuss site security.

• Which things get stolen from building sites?

• Which types of building site are most at risk?

• How is theft prevented on building sites?

• What other things could be done?

Read this advert.

SECURITY FENCING

Building site security fencing is becoming more and more common, particularly on larger construction sites, both to protect the public from potential hazards and to protect expensive tools and materials from thieves.

Safe Site Facilities are able to supply and install numerous types of security fencing within days. Steel security fencing offers a cost-effective security solution, providing a formidable barrier of great strength and rigidity. We can advise on and supply the right site security fencing for you.

 Draft an email to Safe Site Facilities.

- Introduce yourself and explain you are writing on behalf of a construction project that you are working on.

- Briefly describe your building site (you can describe any site you know or have worked on).

- Ask them what kind of fencing they would recommend.

- Share your email with a partner.

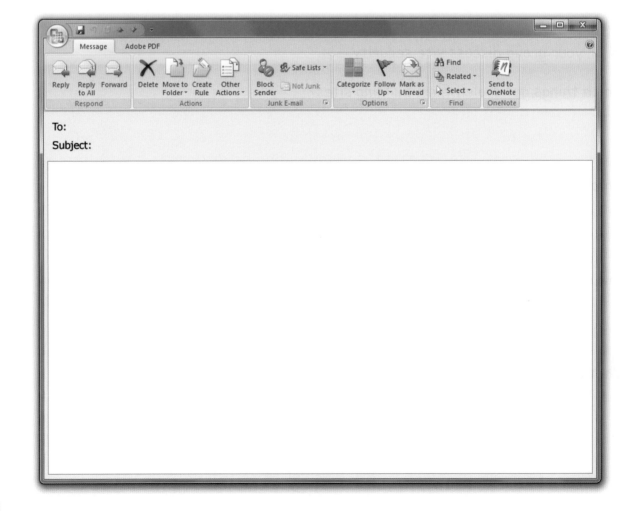

FOCUS ON Apostrophes

There are two ways in which we use apostrophes:

* when letters are missing
* to show possession.

Apostrophes to show that letters are missing

When we deliberately shorten a word or phrase we can use an apostrophe to show that letters are missing. This is also called a 'contraction'.

We use an apostrophe when two words are combined to make one

* For example: 'I am' is shortened to 'I'm'.

A Replace the words in brackets with one word containing an apostrophe.

1 (He is) [＿＿＿＿＿＿＿＿] working on a site in East London.

2 We will not be able to come next week because (we are) [＿＿＿＿＿＿＿＿] busy.

3 (They are) [＿＿＿＿＿＿＿＿] going to come on Tuesday.

We often use an apostrophe to shorten 'have' or 'has'

* For example: 'we have' is shortened to 'we've'.

B Replace the words in brackets with one word containing an apostrophe.

1 (I have) [＿＿＿＿＿＿＿＿] found a source for hand tools.

2 (They have) [＿＿＿＿＿＿＿＿] gone away for two weeks.

3 Dave has given me a leaflet that (he has) [＿＿＿＿＿＿＿＿] written about COSHH.

The word 'not' is often shortened to 'n't' when it is combined with another word

* For example: 'is not' is shortened to 'isn't'.

C Replace the words in brackets with one word containing an apostrophe.

1 The plumber (was not) [____] able to come today.

2 We (were not) [____] expecting the gas engineer.

3 We (cannot) [____] take on any more work at the moment.

4 I (could not) [____] believe how much was wasted.

5 The council (would not) [____] take the building waste.

6 Why (do not) [____] you spend more time with customers?

Note: People often confuse 'you're' and 'your'. 'You're' is short for 'you are', while 'your' means belonging to you. In the same way, 'they're' is short for 'they are', while 'there' is a place. If you are not sure, say it in full.

The possessive apostrophe

A lot of people are confused by the possessive apostrophe. Some people try to overcome the problem by putting an apostrophe after any 's' at the end of a word!

It is called the possessive apostrophe because it is used when writing about something that belongs to, or is owned by, a person, place or thing.

An apostrophe followed by 's' ('s) is added to singular words (i.e. where there is only one person, place or thing)

• For example: my neighbour's bin = the bin belonging to my neighbour.

D Put the apostrophe in the correct place below.

Her friends old clothes. (One friend)

If the word is plural and already ends with an 's', then you just add an apostrophe

• For example: her friends' old clothes = the old clothes belonging to her friends. (More than one friend)

E Put the apostrophe in the correct place below.

The boys room. (More than one boy)

An apostrophe followed by 's' ('s) is added to plural words that do not end with an 's'

• For example: the children's toys = the toys belonging to the children.

F Put the apostrophe in the correct place below.

The mens equipment.

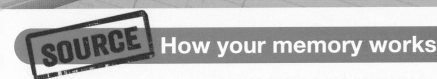
SOURCE How your memory works

The brain

Your brain is like an amazing computer that stores memories and information. There are two types of memory.

Short-term memory holds a small amount of information for a short period of time. It makes particular use of the part of your brain called the 'pre-frontal lobe'.

Long-term memory stores an unlimited amount of information indefinitely.

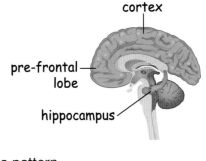
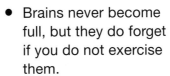
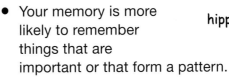

Facts

- Brains never become full, but they do forget if you do not exercise them.
- Your memory is more likely to remember things that are important or that form a pattern.
- Different parts of the same memory are stored in different parts of your brain.
- Most human beings find handwriting, speech and faces easy to remember.

cortex

pre-frontal lobe

hippocampus

Information is transferred from short-term to long-term memory through a special part of the brain. This part of the brain, called the 'hippocampus', is like a sorting centre where new sensations are compared with previous ones.

When we remember new facts by repeating them or using other memory techniques we are actually passing them through the hippocampus several times. This keeps strengthening the associations among these new elements until the brain has learned to associate these things to create what we call a memory.

The hippocampus is important in what is called **episodic memory**. This lets you remember something years later, like a happy holiday. It allows you to 'play the scene back' by restarting the pattern of the activity in the various parts of the brain.

How to improve your memory

Here are some tips on how to improve your memory:

- **Repetition:** this is the best way to remember things for a short period of time, such as a phone number or ingredients for a recipe.
- **Make up a story:** if you have to remember a list of things, create a story that includes them all. This will make connections between them and you will remember them better.
- **Mental exercise:** games, puzzles and mental arithmetic are like 'brain aerobics'.
- **Physical exercise:** this increases your heart rate and sends more oxygen to your brain, which makes your memory work better.
- **Listen to music:** research shows that listening to relaxing instrumental music helps you to organise ideas more clearly and remember things better.
- **Eat the right things:** food containing omega-3, such as fish, spinach and olive oil, helps to improve your memory. Vitamins C and E (in oranges, strawberries and red grapes) and vitamin B (in meat and green vegetables) are also good for your brain.
- **Control stress:** relaxing, getting enough sleep and positive thinking also help your memory.

A Read the text and answer these questions.

1 What type of memory stores information for a short period?

2 Which part of the brain compares previous sensations with new ones?

3 Name one type of thing that most human beings find easy to remember.

4 What is the best way to remember things for a short time?

5 What sends more oxygen to the brain and makes your memory work better?

6 Name a food that contains omega-3.

B What do you remember or forget?

1 Make a note of what you need to remember:

a) at home

b) at college

c) at work.

2 What do you do to help you remember?

3 What do you tend to forget?

Share your list with a partner.

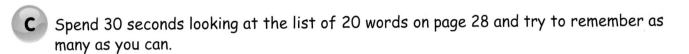

C Spend 30 seconds looking at the list of 20 words on page 28 and try to remember as many as you can.

Now write all of the words that you remember here.

- If you remembered at least five, that is good.
- What methods did you use to remember them?
- Did you try making up a story to connect the words?

D Look at the words you wrote down. Did you spell them all correctly?

Jot down here any that you got wrong and try to learn them. Then have another go.

E Write a story to help you remember these words.

work   sandwich   hat   empty   pink   inside   shirt   angry   umbrella   fly

F I went on holiday.

This is a group game for 4 to 10 players.

The first person says, 'I went on holiday and I took ...'

They follow this by saying something they might take on holiday, for example, sunglasses.

The second person says, 'I went on holiday and I took some sunglasses and ...', adding another item, such as a beach towel.

Each person has to remember all of the things that have been said before and add a new one at the end.

If someone forgets an item then they have to drop out.

Play goes on until only one person is left.

Words to remember for Activity C:

fish	blue	five	hand	bucket
sad	today	tall	dress	why
banana	eat	boat	tree	silly
fiddlesticks	wall	star	chair	sleep

Keeping safe on roofs

All work on roofs is highly dangerous, even if a job only takes a few minutes.

- It is **high-risk** work: almost one in five deaths in construction involve roof work. They include specialist roofers but also others who are repairing and cleaning roofs.
- The **main causes** of death and injury are falling from roof edges or openings, or through fragile roofs or rooflights.
- Many accidents could be avoided if the most suitable **equipment** was used and **people** had the right information, instruction, training and supervision.

Building firms must take proper precautions to control the risk and train their workers about these precautions. A 'method statement' is the common way to help manage work on roofs and communicate the precautions to those involved.

Safe access

Safe access to a roof requires careful planning. Typical methods to access roofs are:

- general access scaffolds
- stair towers, fixed or mobile scaffold towers

- mobile access equipment
- ladders
- roof access hatches.

Roof edges and openings

Falls from roof edges occur on both of the following:

- Sloping roofs: you must use scaffolding to prevent people or materials falling from the edge. You must also fit edge protection to the eaves of any roof and on both front and rear roofs of terraced properties. Where a job takes a few minutes you can use properly secured ladders to access the roof and proper roof ladders.
- Flat roofs: falls from flat roof edges can be prevented by using a secure double guard rail and toeboard around the edge.

Fragile surfaces

- Treat all roofs as fragile until a competent person has confirmed they are not.
- Always follow a safe system of work on fragile roofs. If possible, use a platform beneath the roof. If you must work on the roof itself, use a combination of stagings, guard rails, fall restraint, fall arrest and safety nets slung beneath and close to the roof.
- Do not trust any sheeted roof, whatever the material, to bear a person's weight. This includes the roof ridge and purlins.
- Fragile rooflights are a particular hazard. Some are difficult to see in certain light conditions and others may be hidden by paint. You must provide protection in these areas, by using barriers or covers that are labelled with a warning.

A With a partner, discuss the following words and write down what they mean.

1	Risk	
2	Rooflight	
3	Purlins	
4	Guard rail	

B Read the text and answer these questions.

1 Who is the text 'Keeping safe on roofs' written for?

2 What is the purpose of the text?

3 What proportion of deaths in construction involve roof work?

4 What do you think a 'method statement' is?

5 Give two examples of ways to access a roof.

a)

b)

C Match the type of roof to the precaution.

Type of roof		Precaution	
1	Sloping roof	a)	Never trust this type of roof to bear a person's weight.
2	Flat roof	b)	Use a platform beneath the roof where possible.
3	Fragile roof	c)	Use scaffolding to prevent people or materials falling from the edge.
4	Sheeted roof	d)	Use a secure double guard rail and toeboard around the edge.

D With a partner, read this case study and answer the questions below.

Gwyndaf Davies was helping to re-roof a building in Carmarthenshire. The roof had limited edge protection and no precautions to prevent someone falling through the roof. Gwyndaf fell through the roof to the concrete floor below, suffering multiple spine and facial fractures, as well as a traumatic brain injury.

Gwyndaf spent nine months as an in-patient at Morriston Hospital and has undergone significant facial reconstructive surgery and eye surgery.

The accident has left Gwyndaf with the lasting effects of a traumatic brain injury. He has limited speech, is blind in one eye and partially sighted in the other, and cannot walk without aid. He continues to receive intensive physiotherapy and speech therapy, and it is likely he will need significant care for the rest of his life.

1 What was Gwyndaf doing that led to his injuries?

2 Write down two injuries that Gwyndaf suffered.

a)

b)

3 What three long-term effects has the accident had on Gwyndaf?

a)

b)

c)

 E In your group, discuss working on roofs.

- Have you ever had to work on a roof?
- Do you know other people who have worked on roofs?
- What precautions do companies take to protect people working on roofs?
- Should they take more precautions?

F Choose the correct word to fill the gap in each sentence.

possible   ladders   employers   statement   traumatic   rooflights

1   The law requires all [_____] and contractors to assess the risks of work on roofs.

2   Avoid working on roofs wherever [_____].

3   Use a method [_____] to help manage work on roofs.

4   For jobs that take just a few minutes you can use proper roof [_____].

5   Risks of working on roofs include roof edges or openings, fragile roofs and [_____].

6   Gwyndaf Davies suffered multiple spine and facial fractures, as well as a [_____] brain injury.

G Work with a partner to plan a poster warning of the dangers of working on roofs.

FOCUS ON Non-verbal communication

Non-verbal communication (NVC) is any type of behaviour that is not speech. It is a very powerful communication tool. We are often unaware of the NVC we use.

NVC can be as important as what we say when we are speaking or listening to another person.

Being conscious of your own NVC, and being able to interpret that of others, can help us to understand ourselves and others better.

NVC includes:

- body language
- vocal signals
- personal presentation.

Body language includes a wide range of things such as facial expression, gestures with hands, arms or legs, posture and eye contact.

Vocal signals mean the tone or pitch of your voice when speaking as well as sounds such as 'Mmmm', 'Aha' and 'Er'. These show that you are listening.

 A Match each form of NVC to its possible meaning.

NVC		Possible meaning	
1	Sitting with arms crossed	a)	Agreement
2	Tight lips	b)	Open and welcoming
3	Raised eyebrows	c)	'I do not understand'
4	Slumped in a chair	d)	Bored, not interested
5	Raised voice	e)	Disagreement
6	Arms by sides, relaxed posture	f)	Rejection, defensive
7	Walking with head up	g)	Disbelief or sarcasm
8	Nodding	h)	Anger or fear
9	'Er ...'	i)	Confident

B Think about how a construction worker can use NVC positively when interacting with clients. Write your ideas for each type of NVC.

1 Facial expression

2 Gesture

3 Posture

4 Eye contact

5 Tone of voice

C Look at the examples of NVC below. Circle the ones that you think you use frequently.

touching your nose   hands clasped behind head   smiling   tapping fingers

crossing arms   crossing legs   standing up straight   nodding   frowning

avoiding eye contact   making eye contact   hands on hips   tight or pursed lips

Ask a friend if they agree with you.

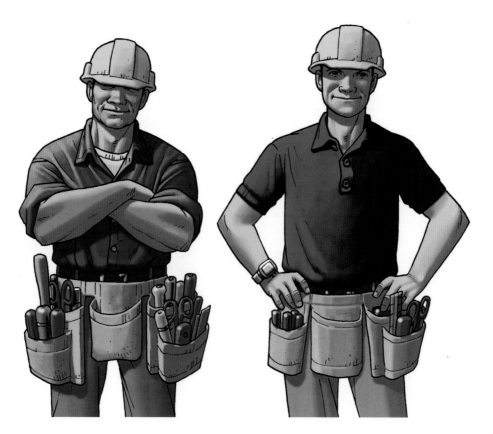

No more waste

Plans have been drawn up to build a new health and social care centre at a cost of approximately £7m. Before starting construction, a cost and benefit analysis was carried out to improve waste management. This is important in two ways:

- It is good for the environment as it will mean that less waste goes to landfill.
- It can save costs in building the health centre.

The health centre will be built on the site of a primary school which is about to be demolished. It will be a large building, three storeys high. The study found that there was a potential saving of £22,985 if the waste reduction plan was implemented.

The study identified the top opportunities for reducing, reusing and recycling waste and estimated how much could be saved by implementing these measures.

Construction materials are a valuable resource. But often there are high levels of

waste through things such as damage on the site, ordering too many materials and the need to redo work if it is not done properly. Reducing this waste saves money.

Waste disposal also costs money. The less waste you have, the less you need to dispose of. Separating waste into different types and finding destinations other than landfill will save money. The analysis found that using three skips instead of one, and separating waste, could save £13,630 of the cost of building the health centre.

Reducing waste to save money

No one wants money to be spent unnecessarily. In the healthcare sector, money saved on costs such as building could be used to improve or add to services.

These were the recommendations from the analysis about how to save money:

- The client needs to instruct the architects of the building to look for waste reduction opportunities.
- The architects need to look for opportunities to design out waste, for example by simplifying the specification.
- The amount of waste produced should be reduced by strategies such as avoiding over ordering and reducing offcuts.
- The cost of waste disposal can be reduced, firstly by producing less waste and also by finding ways to avoid waste going to landfill.
- The waste management contractor must ensure that the waste they receive is recycled wherever possible.

A Choose the correct answer each time.

1 On which site is the new health and social care centre being built?

   a) A landfill site ☐

   b) An old primary school site ☐

   c) A waste management site ☐

2 Using three skips instead of one and separating waste could save:

   a) £13,630 ☐

   b) £22,630 ☐

   c) £22,985 ☐

3 How can architects design out waste?

   a) Recycling waste ☐

   b) Simplifying the specification ☐

   c) Redoing work that is not done properly ☐

4 What should the waste management contractor ensure?

   a) Waste reduction opportunities are identified ☐

   b) Ordering and offcuts are reduced ☐

   c) The waste they receive is recycled wherever possible ☐

B Write down answers to these questions.

1 How much will it cost to build the new health and social care centre?

   [   ]

2 What are the two reasons why the cost and benefit analysis is important?

   a) [   ]

   b) [   ]

3 Give two examples of waste of construction materials.

   a) [   ]

   b) [   ]

4 How can the money saved on building be spent?

   [   ]

C In your group discuss waste. You could make notes below.

- How do the construction organisations that you know reduce waste?

- How might they be able to reduce waste further?

D With a partner, decide where to put commas in these sentences.

1 Before starting construction a cost and benefit analysis was carried out.

2 The less waste you have the less you need to dispose of.

3 Using three skips instead of one and separating waste could save £13,630.

4 Ways of reducing waste include designing out waste simplifying the specification and reducing offcuts.

5 Building firms can help the environment by ordering only what they need reusing old materials creating less waste and recycling more.

E Fill in the gaps in these sentences using the following words:

waste   demolition   bulk   facility   industry   reducing

1 The UK construction [   ] produces over 36 million tonnes of landfill waste each year.

2 Take waste to a local recycling [   ].

3 Reducing [   ] means that less goes to landfill.

4 You can reduce packaging waste by buying in [   ].

5 Some [   ] waste can be reused as aggregates.

6 You can save money by [   ] waste.

F Draw a mind map here to show ways of reducing waste in construction.

Mind maps are a good way of organising the main points for a piece of writing. To create a mind map, write the topic in the centre of the page (for this example, it is 'Reducing waste') and then draw lines to join it to other ideas (e.g. recycling). You can add further lines and detail.

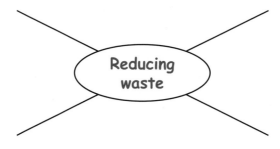

G Use your mind map to help you draft a one-sided leaflet about reducing waste in construction.

SOURCE **Building a renewable future**

Sleaford construction company lands £9.5m energy plant contract

A construction company has been awarded a £9.5m contract to work on the new Renewable Energy Plant in Sleaford.

North Midland Construction plc (NMC) was awarded the contract for the second straw-fired power station in the UK.

The new plant will include two 0.75 acre straw barns, a woodchip import facility, combined turbine and boiler halls as well as administration buildings. The external works for the 10 acre site include sustainable drainage solutions, roads and facilities to export the electricity generated. Surplus heat will be piped to Sleaford's public swimming pool and some other community facilities in the town.

Business development director at NMC, Stuart Campbell, said, 'We're delighted to be involved in such an innovative project that will have a positive impact, not just on the environment but also on the local economy through the creation of jobs in the plant and through the supply chain. We have experience working with the power industry, and renewable energy projects are a fast-growing area for our business as alternative energy remains high on the national infrastructure agenda.'

The Sleaford Renewable Energy Plant will use straw, sourced mainly from local farms, to generate 38 MW of recovered energy. This is enough to provide power and heat for around 65,000 homes.

The plant will save around 250,000 tonnes of CO_2 emissions every year. Ash from the plant

will be recycled for use as fertiliser on farmland. The new renewable energy plant is also expected to create 80 permanent jobs and will provide local straw contracts of up to £10m per year. The plant is due to start operating in 2014.

North Kesteven District Council leader Councillor Marion Brighton said: 'The transfer of free heat will benefit all residents in Sleaford and the surrounding areas, as well as visitors to the town's leisure facilities. It is part of a significant package of benefits, which includes in excess of £200,000 of fresh investment to support our long-term plans to make the district a more sustainable place to live.

'It is important to recognise that the heat being transferred, initially to these three leisure facilities, is a positive by-product of the generation of green electricity. It will make a key contribution to the Council's aims for reducing carbon emissions from public buildings.'

A Read the text and choose the correct answer.

1 What is the value of the new contract?

a) £3.5m ☐

b) £6.5m ☐

c) £9.5m ☐

2 What is the size of the plant site?

a) 0.75 acres ☐

b) 10 acres ☐

c) 38 acres ☐

3 What will be used to generate electricity?

a) Gas ☐

b) Wood ☐

c) Straw ☐

4 Where will surplus heat be piped to?

a) Sleaford's public swimming pool ☐

b) North Kesteven District Council ☐

c) Sleaford Town Council ☐

5 How many homes could be heated by the energy plant?

a) 65,000 ☐

b) 200,000 ☐

c) 250,000 ☐

B Read the text and answer these questions.

1 What impact will the new plant have on the local economy?

2 Give two examples of how waste from the plant will be used.

a)

b)

3 How many tonnes of CO_2 emissions will be saved each year?

C Decide whether each of these statements are presented in the text as facts or opinions.

1 North Midland Construction plc was awarded a £9.5 million contract.   Fact ☐   Opinion ☐

2 The Renewable Energy Plant is an innovative project.   Fact ☐   Opinion ☐

3 The Renewable Energy Plant will use straw sourced mainly from local farms.   Fact ☐   Opinion ☐

4 The plant will benefit all of the residents in Sleaford.   Fact ☐   Opinion ☐

5 The plant will save around 250,000 tonnes of CO_2 emissions every year.   Fact ☐   Opinion ☐

D Suggest two examples from the text that show it might be biased.

a)

b)

E Discuss renewable energy construction projects in your group.

- What kinds of renewable energy construction projects are there?
- What benefits can they have?
- What disadvantages can there be?
- Would you like to work on a project like this? Why?

F Names of things such as people, places, brands and organisations start with a capital letter wherever they appear in a sentence.

Look at the phrases below. Underline the words that should start with a capital letter.

1 north midland construction

2 north kesteven district council

3 straw-fired power station

4 sleaford renewable energy plant

5 combined turbine and boiler halls

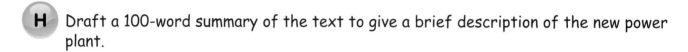

G Read the text again and identify the main points that it contains.

You can do this in several ways. For example, you can:

- use a highlighter pen or underline key phrases or sentences
- cross out sentences (or paragraphs) that you will not need
- make notes of key words and phrases.

H Draft a 100-word summary of the text to give a brief description of the new power plant.

The original article is nearly 400 words long and your task is to cut it down to around 100 words.

1   In the space below or on a separate piece of paper, make notes of the main points.

2   Read the article again to check that you have included all of the main points.

3   Write up your summary, using your notes rather than the original article – this will help you to use your own words where possible.

I Check what you have written.

- Is the length right (around 100 words)?
- Have you included all of your main points?
- Is the summary clear and concise?
- Is the punctuation and spelling OK?

Make any changes you wish to make.

FOCUS ON Commas

There are a number of places where we need to use commas. The main ones are:

- in lists
- to separate parts of sentences
- to replace brackets.

We will look at these in turn.

Commas in a list

We use commas to separate items in a list.

- For example: The budget included materials costs, labour costs and other costs.

 A Add commas to separate items in these sentences.

1   Sheet materials include plywood plasterboard chipboard and MDF.

2   When comparing suppliers you need to consider price quality and delivery.

3   The site team included electricians plumbers bricklayers carpenters and plasterers.

4   Chemicals on site include paint varnish thinners white spirit and primers.

Separating parts of sentences

We also use a comma to separate two parts of a sentence. Often the comma marks off introductory words.

- For example: Despite the rain, we were able to finish work on the roof.

Sometimes the comma and a linking word such as 'but' or 'although' join two sentences together.

- For example: Most injuries in construction are caused by falls from a height, but many injuries are also caused by slips or falls on a level surface.

 B Add commas to separate the two parts of these sentences.

1   The larger the project the more trades will likely be involved.

2   In construction moving and handling account for 8 per cent of major injuries.

3   To reduce the manual handling risk follow safe lifting procedures.

4   Following a meeting with the client the conservatory was made 50mm higher.

Commas instead of brackets

In this case two commas mark off part of a sentence.

* For example: David Lawton, site agent, can give you more details.

C Add two commas to each of these sentences.

1 CIRIA the Construction Industry Research and Information Association offers business improvement services to members.

2 Lisa Ross chief executive said this would never happen again.

3 There is an increasing demand in both the public and private sectors for more sustainable construction.

4 The Code for Sustainable Homes an environmental rating system for housing sets standards for energy efficiency.

Getting a feel for commas

If you are not sure about whether to use a comma, try reading the sentence aloud. If you feel you need to pause, you may need a comma (as in this sentence).

D Read this passage out loud, and decide where best to put commas.

Dermatitis can occur quickly after contact with a strong irritant or over a longer period from repeated contact with weaker irritants. If someone develops an allergy this may become permanent so that any future contact with the substance may cause an allergic reaction. In building work dermatitis can be caused by many things including wet cement solvents and dusts.

E Write three sentences here. Then read them out aloud. Do you need to use commas?

1

2

3

Time on your hands

Managing time is important for both your work and your studies. It helps you to get the right balance between your work and personal life.

In construction there are always time pressures. Deadlines are tight, and you may need to complete one task before someone else can start work on theirs. You may need to cope with unexpected crises. Delays at one stage can have a major impact on the success of a project. You may have more than one job on the go at a time, in which case you need to balance the needs of different clients.

The starting point for managing your time is having clear priorities. What are the things that really matter? It is easy to spend too much time on the urgent things that keep cropping up every day and to lose sight of the more important jobs. So make sure you know what is most important. It can help to talk to your supervisor or tutor about this.

One helpful way of keeping yourself organised is to make a list of the things you need to do in the day. This gives you a clear idea of how much you need to do and how much time you can allow for each task. It is also satisfying when you start ticking off the jobs you have finished.

If you have a big task to do, such as an assignment, try breaking it down into smaller tasks. According to the saying, the way to eat an elephant is one bite at a time!

Managing time does not always mean doing things quickly. It is always worth taking the time to do a job well. This can save time in the end as you do not waste time having to do something again because you rushed it the first time.

At the same time, make sure you have breaks during the day. If you have a lunch break and, ideally, get out for some fresh air or exercise, you will come back fresher and with more energy.

A Which of these statements are true and which are false, according to the article?

1 It is important to be clear about your priorities.   True ☐   False ☐

2 Unexpected problems help you to manage time.   True ☐   False ☐

3 It is easy to spend too much time on urgent things.   True ☐   False ☐

4 It is a good idea to work through your lunch break.   True ☐   False ☐

5 It is always worth taking the time to do a job well.   True ☐   False ☐

B Write down answers to these questions.

1 Why is time management important?

2 What is the starting point for time management?

3 What is a helpful way of keeping organised?

4 Give two ways in which a to-do list can help.

a)

b)

5 What is it good to do in your lunch break?

In a group, discuss your own time management.

Below are some of the things that can make it harder to manage your time.

- Which are true for you?
- Which are true for other people?
- Who has good ideas to avoid these problems?

Which of these things do you do?	Often	Sometimes	Never
Leave things until the last minute			
Forget to do important things			
Find it hard to say 'No'			
Spend time on things that do not matter			
Spend too much time on the phone			
Spend too much time on Facebook			
Get distracted easily			

 Fill in the gaps in this paragraph using these words:

list   break   important   organised   distracted   priority   smaller

It is important to know which of your tasks are top [   ] . Find time

for the things that are [   ] but not urgent. If you keep a to-do

[   ] , this will help you to stay [   ] . Make sure

you take a [   ] during the day as this will help you to stay fresh.

Avoid getting [   ] by things that are not important. Break up big jobs

into [   ] tasks as this can make them more manageable.

E Work with a partner. Discuss three ways in which you could manage time better.

1

2

3

 F Write a to-do list below.

1 Make a list here of things that you need to do this week.

2 Which are the most important?

Teamwork

Teamwork and partnership working is very important in construction. This is because a range of people from different trades need to play a part in most building projects.

A definition of a team is:

People working together to achieve a common goal or mission. Their work is interdependent and team members share responsibility for achieving the results.

You will work in a team with your colleagues, and you may work in partnership with other trades. Many building projects include architects, surveyors, estimators, engineers, electricians, plumbers, bricklayers, carpenters, plasterers and other trades.

The key principles of effective teamwork are:

- having shared or common goals
- openness and honesty
- trust and respect
- reliability and commitment.

Effective teams

Here are four characteristics of effective teams – and what can happen if they are not in place.

An effective team has:
- a strong sense of purpose and shared goals
- clear roles and responsibilities
- clear procedures that everyone understands
- good relationships between team members.

If this is not in place:
- there will be reduced effort and low energy
- there is less accountability and more conflict
- more time and effort will be needed to achieve tasks
- it will result in tension and stress and there will be less focus on the goals and tasks.

Communication

Good communication is essential to the smooth running of teams. It provides the basis for positive interpersonal relationships and ensures that goals and procedures are clear. There are two ways in which team members or partnership workers communicate with each other:

- Orally, by speaking and listening. In spoken communication, tone of voice and body language are as important as what we actually say.
- In writing, through instructions, notes and emails. Written communication needs to be clear so that the message cannot be misunderstood.

A Make a list of the teams and partners you work with.

Share your list with a partner or the rest of your group.

B Read the text and answer these questions.

1 What can happen if a team does not have clear procedures?

2 Name two things that are important in oral communication.

a)

b)

3 What can cause a team to lack energy and make less effort?

4 Give an example of a building trade mentioned in the text

5 Why is good communication important in teamwork?

C When an ending, or suffix, is added to a word, sometimes the word stays the same and sometimes the final letter 'e' is removed.

- For example:
  - argue, argument, arguing
  - enhance, enhancement, enhancing

Add 'ment' and 'ing' to these words.

Word	+ ment	+ ing
1 achieve		
2 treat		
3 encourage		
4 require		
5 appoint		
6 amaze		

 D For each of the following words, write a sentence that contains that word.

1 Reliability

2 Accountable

3 Tension

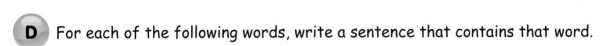 **E** Read the case study and answer the questions below.

Case study: Organising the building site

The site management team is led by the contracts manager who is based in head office and is responsible for planning the job and solving larger problems that come up. The site agent manages the job on a day-to-day basis, and is responsible for managing the team and resources. The site engineer checks that the building is being constructed correctly. Teams for each trade (electricians, plumbers, bricklayers, carpenters, plasterers) are managed by supervisors who are responsible to the general foreman, who in turn reports to the site agent. The general foreman holds daily meetings with the trade supervisors and also meets weekly with the site agent and contracts manager to discuss how the job is going.

1 What is the role of the contracts manager?

2   What is the role of the site manager?

3   What is the role of the site engineer?

4   Which meetings is the general foreman involved in?

5   Fill in the gaps below to show who is responsible to who:

Carpenter → [   ] → [   ] → [   ]
→ Contracts manager

F Write a short note describing what the team you work in does that makes it effective.

FOCUS ON **Questions**

It may seem obvious what a question is, but people are often not sure when a question mark is needed.

A question is a statement that asks for information. For example:

• Where do you work?

• Which chisel should I use for this job?

A Look at the statements below. Put either a question mark or a full stop at the end of each line.

1 What is the budget for the project

2 The deadline is 24 May

3 When can we start work

4 When will the scaffolding be installed

5 The skip will be delivered on Tuesday morning

6 How long will the plaster take to dry

Question words

Some words are used regularly at the start of a question, such as 'why', 'when', 'who', 'how', 'where' and 'what'.

B Insert a word at the start of these statements to make them questions.

1 [   ] is your favourite food?

2 [   ] is your appointment with the doctor?

3 [   ] do you live?

4 [   ] time do you need to catch the bus?

5 [   ] does she manage to do so much?

Asking questions

In construction you will need to ask a lot of questions! You will often have to be careful about how you phrase them.

For example, if a member of the public is standing too close to where you are working, you could ask: 'Can you stand somewhere else?'

But it is more polite to say: 'Please can you stand a little further away?'

Wording your question in this way is more polite and sounds more like a request than a demand or instruction.

C Try wording these requests more tactfully.

1 What do you want to drink?

2 Will you put that down? You will break it.

3 Give me the materials specification.

Open and closed questions

There are two types of questions: 'open' and 'closed' questions.

Closed questions often invite 'yes' or 'no' or very brief answers. They do not open up a conversation, but they are good for checking details.

- For example: 'Have you checked the delivery?'

An open question needs a longer answer, allowing someone to give you more information or tell you how they think and feel. Open questions often start with 'how', 'what', 'which' and 'why'.

- For example: 'What did the delivery contain?'

D Rewrite these closed questions as open questions.

1 Did your meeting go well?

2 Do you like working on the new site?

3 Have you had a good day?

This does not mean you should not use closed questions. They are useful for finding out precise facts or checking information.

The fireplace specialist

Toby was a customer service manager and he really wasn't enjoying his job, so he decided to change his career. He enjoyed practical work and had read that plumbers were earning more than airline pilots, so he thought that sounded like a good idea!

He was taken on as a labourer with a heating engineer. It turned out that this engineer was more of a fireplace specialist and Toby found this area of work very interesting. The engineer took him on as an apprentice and he spent three years learning about heating engineering as well as fireplace installation.

After Toby qualified he carried on working for the engineer for about a year and then worked for a fireplace shop before setting up as a self-employed fireplace specialist. Fireplace work varies, but there are two main fields:

- **Flue specialists** deal with problem flues and leaking flues, installing flue linings and wood-burning stoves.

- **Fireplace specialists** install new and replacement fireplaces, mainly in private homes. They need to ensure fireplaces function safely. They also have to know the regulations about fireplace materials and how to use them and understand stone and how to handle it.

Here is how Toby describes what his job involves.

'A job can involve anything from taking out a whole fireplace and doing a complete replacement to replacing the firebricks or grate. I also do a lot of jobs where I'm reusing original materials, so I need to be able to put together broken parts or restore fire surrounds. I am often asked to install reproduction fireplaces – these are mainly Victorian because a lot of the houses in the area are of that period. The starting point varies, it could be a completely bricked-up chimney breast or an open chamber. Sometimes the original surrounds are in pieces and I have to reassemble and restore them using authentic materials.

'A lot of the fires I install and work on are decorative gas fires. These are very popular as they don't need cleaning out every time they're used and people don't have to buy supplies of logs or coal. They have come a long way in recent years; they are more efficient, safer and give off more heat.'

Toby has no difficulty getting enough work. He is commissioned to carry out installations by a number of shops that sell fireplaces, as well as getting direct requests from individual homeowners. He really enjoys what he does because it involves a wide range of skills – plumbing, plastering and rendering, pipework and general building.

A Read the case study and answer these questions.

1 What job did Toby do before he started training as a heating engineer?

2 List two things a flue specialist does.

a)

b)

3 Where does a fireplace specialist work most of the time?

4 Give two reasons why people prefer decorative gas fires.

a)

b)

5 List two ways in which gas fires have improved.

a)

b)

6 List two of the skills Toby uses in his work.

a)

b)

B Match the words below with their meanings.

Words	Meaning
1 Authentic	a) The act of putting a piece of equipment or machinery into place
2 Decorative	b) Genuine and original
3 Installation	c) Something that is attractive rather than functional

C Do you think that being a fireplace specialist sounds like an interesting job? Discuss in a group.

• What skills do you already have that are relevant?

• What skills would you need to develop?

D In your group discuss the parts of the job that you think you would like and those which you would not be keen on.

E The text contains a number of words that begin with the prefix 're-' For example, Toby **restores** and **replaces** fireplaces. He sometimes has to **reassemble** them or put in **reproduction** ones.

Find a word beginning with 're-' to fill the gap in each of the sentences below.

1 The electrics in the house were in a terrible state so we had to completely

[   ] them.

2 I had to [   ] my electric drill because the battery was flat.

3 The wallpaper is peeling and the paintwork is in a bad state, so we will need to

[   ] the room.

4 The customer complained about the standard of work and asked us to

[   ] the job.

F Read the information about HETAS and choose the correct answer to each question.

HETAS | Always use a HETAS registered installer

HETAS stands for Heating Equipment Testing and Approval Scheme. It is the official body recognised by the government to approve biomass and solid fuel domestic heating appliances, fuels and services, including the registration of competent installers and servicing businesses.

HETAS registered installers have been assessed for competence in the installation of solid fuel and biomass appliances. Registered competent installers can self-certify their installations.

It is the leading training provider for solid fuel, wood and biomass courses, specifically designed for installers, chimney sweeps, retailers and others. Successful completion of the three-day course HETAS Dry Appliance Installer leads to certification of competence. To be accepted for the course you need to have knowledge and understanding of building regulations and working experience in the construction and/or heating industry.

1 What is HETAS?

a) A private training organisation ☐

b) An official body recognised by the government ☐

c) A company that installs heating appliances ☐

2 How long is the training course for installers?

   a) Three days ☐

   b) Three months ☐

   c) Three years ☐

3 Who can do the course?

   a) Anyone who is interested ☐

   b) Only qualified heating engineers ☐

   c) People who know about building regulations and have experience in construction or heating ☐

G Fill the gaps in the text using the following words:

fuels   appliances   atmosphere   renewable   matter
registered   sustainable   energy   wood

Due to rising _____ costs, appliances that burn biomass _____ are becoming more popular. The term 'biomass' refers to any organic _____ that can be used as fuel. The most common biomass fuel is _____ in the form of logs, wood pellets or wood chips. Wood is one of the best sources of _____ energy for heating. As long as you buy your fuel from a _____ source you will not increase the levels of carbon dioxide in the _____. Biomass _____ must be installed by a HETAS _____ installer.

When you have finished, read the text through to ensure it makes sense.

H Write a paragraph that includes the following words:

appliance   energy   expensive   heating

Health and safety for smaller builders

The Health and Safety Executive (HSE) website contains advice for smaller builders about carrying out projects safely.

The HSE uses the term 'smaller builder' to describe contractors who undertake work on the following:

- **Private domestic projects** – involving extensions, repairs and refurbishment work on private homes. The small builder has the sole responsibility for site health and safety on these projects.
- **Smaller business projects** – involving short-duration repairs and refurbishment work for business clients (fewer than 30 days of construction work), where site safety responsibilities are shared between small builders and the business client.

Most fatal injuries in the construction industry now occur on smaller building projects involving refurbishment of existing homes and workplaces. Over 60 per cent of those deaths involve falls from ladders, scaffolds, working platforms and roof edges and falls through fragile roofs or rooflights.

Other fatal injuries on smaller projects are the result of the collapse of excavations, lifting operations, electricity and mobile plant.

Smaller builders must be competent to carry out their work safely. You should not accept work for which you do not have the necessary health and safety competency.

Managing hazards and risk

As a smaller builder, you are a contractor under Construction (Design and Management) Regulations (CDM) 2007. The law requires you to:

- **plan, manage and monitor** construction work so that health and safety risks are controlled
- **set lead times** – inform any subcontractors of the minimum amount of time that will be allowed for planning and preparation

- **prevent site access** – check that steps have been taken to prevent access by unauthorised persons to the site
- **provide information and training** – give your workforce information and training on risks, precautions and rules
- **arrange welfare facilities** – make sure adequate welfare facilities are in place for the workforce.

Cooperating with the client

The business client has legal duties and is obliged to cooperate with you and have arrangements for managing the work.

The home occupier has no responsibility for workplace safety so you should work closely with them to meet your responsibilities for site safety. The smaller builder and occupier have a common interest in making sure the building work does not put residents at risk.

For example, you should ensure that the site is left in a safe condition at the end of the day and that residents are not put at risk while work is in progress. The occupier will need to know about and cooperate with the plans for the work.

A Write down the answers to these questions.

1 What is the purpose of the text 'Health and safety for smaller builders'?

2 What two types of project does a smaller builder work on?

3 On what projects do most fatal injuries in construction occur?

4 Over 60 per cent of deaths are caused by falls from ladders, scaffolds, working platforms, roof edges, falls through fragile roofs and rooflights. What do all of these have in common?

5 Which type of client shares responsibility with the builder for health and safety?

B Prepare for a discussion about health and safety and small builders.

Think about the following questions and make notes about your responses below.

- Did it surprise you that most fatal accidents in construction are on smaller projects?
- What do you think are the reasons for this?
- What do you think are the main differences between health and safety measures in large companies and those in smaller ones?
- What could a small builder do to control risks and reduce accidents?

C Match the legal responsibility for health and safety to the correct method for managing risk.

Legal responsibility		Method for managing risk	
1	Plan and manage work	a)	Site induction, emergency procedures
2	Information and training	b)	Toilets, washing facilities
3	Prevent site access	c)	Carry out risk assessments
4	Workforce welfare	d)	Fence boundaries

D Complete the sentences using your own words to show what might happen if health and safety precautions are not taken.

1 If the people who work on the site do not have access to washing facilities then

2 If the boundaries of the site are not clearly defined

3 If risk assessments are not carried out

E Put commas in the correct places in each sentence.

1 Fatal injuries on small construction projects can be caused by falls lifting operations electricity and mobile plant.

2 Dave a roofer on the project fell from the scaffold and injured his back.

3 Although some small builders take health and safety very seriously others are less conscientious.

4 The workforce should be informed of risks precautions and site rules.

5 To reduce danger to the public make sure the site is fenced off.

F Children often think that a construction site is a fun and safe place to play. They treat the site like a playground for exploring, climbing or playing hide and seek. A number of children die or are seriously injured every year as a result. Read the example below and then answer the questions that follow on page 62.

A game of hide and seek ended in disaster when a nine-year-old girl was seriously injured after trespassing on a construction site. Maddy was with her friend, Alice, when she decided that a pile of timber would make a good hiding place. While searching for her friend, Alice climbed onto the stack, causing it to collapse and trapping Maddy underneath. Alice heard her friend cry out and rang the fire brigade. Firefighters dragged her out just seconds before the rest of the pile crashed down. Maddy was taken to hospital where she was described as 'poorly, but stable'. She could have been killed but was lucky to escape with cuts and bruises and a broken leg.

1   What game were the girls playing?

2   Where did Maddy hide?

3   Who rescued her?

4   What injuries did Maddy sustain?

G   Put the events in the story in the right order by numbering them.

- Alice climbed onto the pile of timber.   ☐
- Alice called the fire brigade.   ☐
- The stack of timber collapsed.   ☐
- Maddy and Alice trespassed on a building site.   ☐
- Maddy was taken to hospital.   ☐
- Maddy hid under a pile of timber.   ☐

H   Draft a leaflet telling children why construction sites are dangerous.

Think about how the leaflet could be designed to gain children's attention.

Share with a partner what you have drafted and then combine the best ideas into one revised draft.

FOCUS ON Audience and purpose

Whenever you say or write anything, you need to be clear about:

- who you are speaking or writing to – your audience
- why you are speaking or writing – your purpose.

This is especially important when you are planning a letter, report, talk or presentation.

Your audience

Things to think about for your audience include:

- who they are and whether you know them already
- why they will read or listen to what you write or say
- what is likely to interest them
- which style is likely to be appropriate or inappropriate
- how much they know about the subject
- whether they will know technical terms
- whether they may have any difficulty listening or reading.

A Who might be the audience for each of these items?

Possible audiences: tutor, manager, fellow students, work colleagues, friends.

1   Assignment for your course

2   Text saying where to meet tonight

3   Talk about a work placement

4   Report about building materials

B Imagine you are writing an assignment for your tutor. Which of these statements are true and which are false?

1 You should use a formal style.   True ☐   False ☐

2 You should make it amusing.   True ☐   False ☐

3 You should have a clear structure.   True ☐   False ☐

4 You should not include technical terms.   True ☐   False ☐

5 You should stick to the topic.   True ☐   False ☐

Your purpose

Common purposes for speaking and writing include to inform, to explain, to impress, to persuade and to entertain.

When you plan a talk or piece of writing, make sure you are clear about your purpose and what you want people to know, understand and do as a result of what they hear or read.

C Who is the audience, and what is the purpose of this text?

People working in construction are exposed to substances that could harm their health. The term for these is 'hazardous substances'. To carry out COSHH risk assessments, employers should think about how each substance is used and for what tasks. They should pay particular attention to any processes that produce dust, vapour, fumes or gas that people could breathe in. They should also look out for substances that come into contact with the skin, such as dusts or liquids.

D Who is the audience, and what is the purpose of this text?

A construction company has been awarded a £9.5m contract to work on the new Renewable Energy Plant in Sleaford. North Midland Construction plc (NMC) was awarded the contract for the second straw-fired power station in the UK. The new plant will include two 0.75 acre straw barns, a woodchip import facility, combined turbine and boiler halls plus administration buildings. Surplus heat will be piped to Sleaford's public swimming pool and some other community facilities in the town.

Give and take

Building work depends on good communication skills. You need to be able to communicate well with clients and customers – but it is also vital to communicate well with your colleagues – the other people you work with.

An important part of being a good communicator is being sensitive to other people. This can involve three key things:

- Respect – which means showing other people that you care about them or value their views by behaving in a respectful way.

- Empathy – which means trying to understand another person's feelings as if they were your own – 'putting yourself in their shoes'.
- Trust – which means showing other people that they can count on you to do what you say you will do, and to support them.

Good communication with colleagues also depends on good information sharing.

- Giving information – you may need to pass on information to someone replacing you at the end of your shift, you may need to report something to your manager, or you may need to pass on a message to another tradesperson. In all of these cases you need to remember to share the information promptly, clearly and accurately.
- Listening carefully to what other people say – you will also receive information from colleagues. You need to listen to what they say and check if you do not understand something.

Bear in mind that several things can get in the way of sharing information. Barriers to communication can result from:

- the way the message is communicated (e.g. using ambiguous words or phrases, using complex technical terms, mumbling or writing badly)
- the way the message is received (e.g. the person listening or reading may be tired, hard of hearing or may not understand the language used)
- the environment (e.g. a noisy room, interruptions from other people, an email not getting through or a crackly mobile phone line).

Good communication also depends on being prepared to ask for help, advice and support when you need it, and being prepared to accept offers of help from colleagues. In turn, you should be prepared and ready to offer help, advice and support when this is appropriate.

A Match these terms to their definitions.

Term	Definition
1 Respect	a) Showing other people that they can count on you
2 Empathy	b) Showing other people that you care about them or value their views
3 Trust	c) Trying to understand another person's feelings as if they were your own

B Write down answers to these questions.

1 Which two groups of people must a construction worker communicate with?

2 From the text, choose three examples of when you need to give information.

a)

b)

c)

3 Write down the three barriers to communication that are mentioned in the text.

a)

b)

c)

C In your group, read this text.

People may not contribute fully to a discussion because they are shy or lack confidence; they may feel they do not know enough about a topic to contribute; or they may be put off because other people dominate the discussion. You can find ways of encouraging them to say things without them feeling threatened.

In your group, discuss:

• things you can do before a discussion to help people participate

• things you can do during the discussion to help everyone feel involved

• things that might discourage people from participating that you should avoid during discussions.

D Reflect on how well the discussion went.

Look at these pairs of statements and decide in each case whether Statement A or B was more true of your group discussion.

Statement A					Statement B
The discussion had a clear focus.	4	3	2	1	The purpose of the discussion was vague.
Everybody participated.	4	3	2	1	One or two people talked most of the time.
The discussion was lively and interesting.	4	3	2	1	The discussion was dull and boring.
The discussion stayed focused on the point.	4	3	2	1	The discussion often wandered off the point.
The discussion moved on from one topic to the next.	4	3	2	1	The discussion got bogged down in one topic.
We covered all of the discussion points.	4	3	2	1	We only covered one or two discussion points.
We ended on time.	4	3	2	1	We went well over time.

 E Read this text with a partner.

Ground rules

Formal discussions need certain rules if they are to work well. Ground rules set out the behaviours that are or are not acceptable in the group. They can include:

- practical rules (e.g. we arrive on time)
- rules about how we work (e.g. we only have one conversation at a time)
- rules about how we interact (e.g. we listen to what each other says).

Ground rules help a group to operate effectively and help to create a positive and constructive atmosphere. If everyone takes part in agreeing the ground rules, they are more likely to follow them than if one person imposes them.

Identify two ways in which you could have helped the discussion go better.

a)

b)

F Use this checklist to help you move discussions forward.

Discussions can get bogged down – you can find yourself spending too much time on one issue and then having to rush through other important topics. Here are some techniques for helping to move a discussion forward.

☐ Give a short summary of what has been said.

☐ Remind the group about the time that is available.

☐ If contributions are not relevant, gently remind people of the topic.

☐ If two or three people are dominating the discussion, invite other people to contribute who have not yet done so.

☐ If you get bogged down on a topic, consider asking one or two people to take this forward after the meeting.

☐ Try to draw a topic to an end by saying, for example, 'It sounds as if we have agreed that ...'.

☐ Encourage the group to move on by saying, for example, 'Should we move on to the next topic now?'

G Write a message.

At times you may need to leave a written message for a colleague or your manager. Read the example below and compose a message to your colleague.

A delivery of timber has been delayed and will now arrive tomorrow morning. You will not be at work when it arrives and you need to leave a message for the person replacing you. It is important that they check the delivery against the order form.

Which power sander?

Choose the right sander to suit the job and your needs.

Orbital sander
A hand-held sander that moves in small circles thousands of times a minute. Useful for things such as removing old paintwork or sanding back rough timber or plaster.

Detail sander
A small and lightweight sander designed for use in areas that other sanders are not able to reach. They usually have a small pointed sanding area that is good for getting into corners or sanding around irregular shapes. Many are supplied with multiple attachments for different applications.

Random orbital sander
Similar to an orbital sander, but the sanding pad rotates as well oscillating at high speed. This ensures that the same sanding pattern is not repeated over and over again. The random element means that the sander can be moved in any direction without scuffing the surface. Speed control allows the user to slow the sander for work on softer materials.

Rotary/disc sanders
A disc sander uses a circular piece of sandpaper that is rotated at high speed. The sandpaper is clamped to a rubber pad that is designed to flex slightly when pressure is applied. These sanders can also be used for polishing and grinding with special attachments.

The sandpaper pads used on this type of sander are prone to tearing if the edges become caught on a sharp edge. This is not such a problem as they are cheap to replace. Scuffing and swirl marks are common when using disc sanders, which means that another, possibly manual, form of sanding is needed to give a smooth finish.

Belt sander
A continuous loop of sandpaper is rotated at high speed around two wheels. A belt sander is best suited for preparation work. They can be hard to control as the belt grips the workpiece and tries to drive away. Useful for reducing timber sizes before smooth sanding.

Palm sander
A palm sander is held with the sanding surface directly under the handle to transfer the user's grip pressure to the sanding surface. These sanders are useful for fine finishing, but can quickly cause fatigue and discomfort due to the vibration. High-end models have superior vibration suppression to eliminate this problem, but it can never be removed completely.

A Read the information about sanders and answer these questions.

1 Which sander has a continuous loop of sandpaper?

2 Which sander uses a circular piece of paper?

3 Which sander reduces the risk of scuffing?

4 What are the disadvantages of a palm sander?

5 Which sander is likely to cause scuffing or swirl marks?

B Write what each sander is used for in the column beside its name.

Sanding irregular shapes   Reducing the size of timber
Removing old paintwork   Fine finishing

Type of sander	Use
Orbital sander	
Belt sander	
Palm sander	
Detail sander	

C Tick the correct answer each time.

1 Which word means to swing between two points in a rhythmic motion?

a) Articulate ☐   b) Oscillate ☐   c) Facilitate ☐

2 Which word means a pattern or sizes that are not regular?

a) Variation ☐   b) Changeable ☐   c) Random ☐

3 Which word means to bend?

a) Flex ☐   b) Rotate ☐   c) Vibrate ☐

D Compare the adverts for the two disc sanders and answer these questions by ticking the correct box.

1 Which sander has the more powerful motor?

a) Axminster AWDS12H ☐

b) Axminster DS12DL ☐

2 Which sander is the more expensive?

a) Axminster AWDS12H ☐

b) Axminster DS12DL ☐

3 Which sander needs adjusting before use?

a) Axminster AWDS12H ☐

b) Axminster DS12DL ☐

4 Which sander uses 300 mm discs?

a) Axminster AWDS12H ☐

b) Axminster DS12DL ☐

c) Both the AWDS12H and the DS12DL ☐

Axminster AWDS12H 300 mm Disc Sander £151.99 Inc. VAT

Key features

- Good value for money disc sander
- Quiet 750 W induction motor
- Brake slows the disc down in a reasonable time
- Heavy-duty handles at both ends
- Dust extractor

Customer review ★★★★

A great machine for the money. Quiet and stable, the cast iron bed needed the rough edges taken off with a file and the fence also needed adjustment to make it run smooth and now it does. Before buying this model I did look at several other makes of 12" disc sander for under £200 and this is by far the better machine.

Axminster DS12DL 300 mm Disc Sander £267.95 Inc. VAT

Key features

- Bench-mounted sander
- Fabricated steel construction throughout
- Simple and positive table adjustments
- Accurate mitre fence
- Well-positioned dust extraction outlet
- 560 W induction motor

Customer review ★★★★

Well worth it!
Follow the golden rule – don't ever operate this without a dust extractor! Also, bolt it down! This machine is solid, vibration is minimal and the disc ran very true. The table is as solid as a rock and will cater for most angles. Go buy one!

E With a partner discuss the merits of each sander. Which one do you think is the 'best buy'?

Agree on three reasons for your choice and write them here.

1

2

3

F In your group, discuss how online reviews can help people to decide what to buy.

Do you think online reviews are reliable and accurate?

G Fill the gaps in the paragraph below using these words:

rapidly   rotate   woodworking   sanders   work
tired   effective   uneven   surface   much

The random orbital sander is one of the best [   ] tools for

removing material from a [   ] quickly. The sanding pads spin and

[   ] in a single movement, making it [   ] in

removing small spots and swirls left by other [   ]. Get the feel

of your sander before you start [   ]. Alternate the position

of your hand to stop it getting [   ]. Keep the sander moving to

avoid an [   ] finish. The sander is designed to remove material

[   ] so try not to remove too [   ] wood at

one time.

FOCUS ON Checking written work

Checking what you have written is really important. It is not just people who struggle with spelling who need to check their work. We all make mistakes without meaning to, especially when using a computer.

Think about publishers – they employ proofreaders to check books before they are printed – even though they have been written by professional writers.

 A Read these tips about how to proofread your work. There are some mistakes, or 'typos'. Underline the ones you find.

Proofreading tips

Profreading is the task of reading and correcting wirtten work. Its best to proofread a paper copy, rather than checking on screen as you will spot erors more easily.

You need to concentrate to do proof reading. Find a quite space where you will not distracted. First, scan your document to make sure the layout is clear Mark anything that looks odd and check pargraphs and headings.

When checking n detail you might put a ruler or peice of paper below the line you are reading to help you focus? Each sentence should start with a capital leter and end with appropriate punctutation such as a fullstop or question mark:

All words must be spelt correct. You can use a dictionery or spellchecker, but you need to be careful with spell checkers as they wont always pick up the right word for the meaning. They will miss spellinh mistakes when a typing error has changed one word ibnto another perfectly good one, such as learner/leaner, where/were, to/too.

B Write the correct spelling of any words that were misspelt.

Which documents need to be checked?

You should check everything you write. Just one missing word in an email to a friend can completely change the meaning or cause confusion, for example if you are making an arrangement to meet. But not everything needs to perfect.

C Tick the documents below that you think need to be thoroughly checked.

☐ A note to your mum saying you have gone out and when you will be back

☐ An email applying for a job

☐ An assignment for your course

☐ An email to a friend

Proofreading checklist

Use this checklist when you proofread an important document.

☐ Scan the whole document – is the layout neat and clear?

☐ Look at the paragraphs – they do not all have to be the same length but are there any that are very long or very short?

☐ Are your headings clear with consistent use of fonts and spacing?

☐ Is the order logical and do the headings help to sequence the content?

☐ Check the titles, captions and position of any tables or illustrations.

☐ Read every sentence and word to look for errors.

☐ Make sure every sentence makes sense and conveys a complete idea.

☐ If you make a correction, read through the whole sentence again to check that it makes sense.

☐ Check sentence punctuation. Do all sentences begin with a capital letter and end with a full stop, question mark or exclamation mark?

☐ Check you have spelt any proper names correctly and used capital letters where they are needed.

☐ If you have used quotations in inverted commas, make sure you have used either single (') or double (") inverted commas consistently.

Ask a friend

It is a good idea to ask someone else to proofread your work. This is because when we check our own work we see what we meant to write rather than what we have actually written. Someone else may spot errors that we miss.

And checking someone else's work will help you to recognise problems and avoid them yourself in the future.

SUCCEEDING IN INTERVIEWS

You should see any sort of job interview as a two-way exchange of information. The interviewer is trying to find out some important things about you – your skills, attitudes, experience and interests – to help them decide whether you are the right person for the job. At the same time you want to find out more about the organisation or company so that you can work out if this is the right job for you.

FIRST IMPRESSIONS REALLY COUNT

It is a sad fact that people form an opinion of someone in the first 10 seconds or so of meeting them. In an interview, that can make a big difference to your chances of getting the job. It can be very difficult to recover from a bad first impression. Below is a breakdown of the importance of three key factors in making a good impression, based on research.

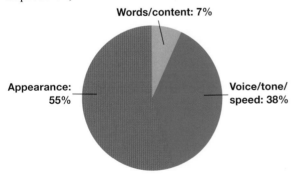

Words/content: 7%
Appearance: 55%
Voice/tone/speed: 38%

In other words, *how* you look and the *way* that you talk are more important than *what* you say!

One aspect of appearance is your body language – how you walk and stand, your gestures and facial expression. Even the interviewer may not be aware that they are responding to this.

USE BODY LANGUAGE WELL

- Smile at the beginning of the interview and look at the interviewer.
- Offer a firm handshake.
- Sit back into your seat. This can help you to look and feel more confident.
- Do not cross your arms – folded arms can make you appear unfriendly and defensive and can be a barrier to communication.
- Maintain regular eye contact with the interviewer but do not stare at them.
- Respond to the interviewer with gestures such as nods and turn towards them to show that you are listening.

THE WAY THAT YOU LOOK

If you search the internet for tips on how to dress for an interview you will find that quite a few sites recommend formal dress (e.g. smart dress/ suit, tie, etc.). But in some sectors, formal clothes may not be appropriate, so the best advice is to choose the most *suitable* clothing. Here are a few tips in terms of appearance:

- Wear clothes in which you feel comfortable and confident.
- Make sure that your clothes are clean and tidy, including your shoes.
- Make sure that you have a bath or shower on the morning of your interview.
- Make sure that you look well groomed. This means neat hair, clean nails, face and so on.
- Do not wear revealing clothes, anything too wacky, too much make-up or jewellery.
- Do not smoke just before an interview – if you feel you must smoke, use a breath freshener.

A Read the text and choose the correct answer.

1 What is the most important factor in making a good impression?

   a) Your tone of voice ☐

   b) What you say ☐

   c) Your appearance ☐

2 Which of the following is a form of body language?

   a) Smiling ☐

   b) Wearing revealing clothes ☐

   c) Smoking ☐

3 How long does it usually take someone to form an opinion of you?

   a) Approximately a minute ☐

   b) About 10 seconds ☐

   c) Five minutes ☐

4 How should you dress for an interview?

   a) You should always wear a jacket or suit. ☐

   b) You should choose suitable clothing. ☐

   c) You should wear clothes that will grab the interviewer's attention. ☐

5 What advice is given about eye contact?

   a) Look the interviewer in the eyes as often as possible. ☐

   b) Do not look the interviewer in the eyes – it is bad manners. ☐

   c) Make regular eye contact but do not stare. ☐

B What are the main 'selling points' that you can offer a potential employer?

- What jobs or work experience have you had?
- What skills and qualifications do you have?
- What equipment can you use?
- What aspects of your personality or attitudes make you a good employee?

C Think of a job that you would like to do.

If you got a job interview tomorrow, what would you wear?

Discuss your answer with a partner.

D Write a short description of a job that you would like to do. It should include:

- the job title
- the organisation or company
- what the job involves
- what skills they are looking for
- what sort of person they are looking for.

E Using the job description you have written, think about how you would answer the following questions in an interview for a job or a work experience placement.

1 What interests you about this job or place of work?

2 How would this job/placement help you with your course or future career?

3 Why are you suitable for this job/placement?

F What you say in an interview matters, but listening effectively can be just as important.

1 Why do you think that listening in an interview is important?

2 How can you use body language to show that you are listening?

G Work in groups of three. Decide on a job that you could all do, or choose one of the job descriptions from Activity D.

Take it in turns to interview each other for the job, with one person acting as interviewer, one as interviewee and one observing. The observer will complete the checklist below.

Start the interview by walking into the room and sitting down. The interviews only need to be about five minutes long. After the interview, discuss your scores with the observer to find out your strengths and weaknesses.

First impressions	✓		✓	Manners
Excellent		5		Charming
Good		4		Agreeable
Satisfactory		3		Satisfactory
Not very good		2		Awkward
Unfavourable		1		Offensive
Oral communication	✓		✓	**Body language**
Excellent choice of words		5		Very effective
Good choice of words		4		Good, positive
Sometimes lost for words		3		Limited, neutral
Limited vocabulary		2		Poor, would not impress
Poor		1		Would create a negative effect

Tips for talking

- [ ] As with appearance, the important thing is to come across as comfortable and natural.
- [ ] Use correct grammar.
- [ ] Speak clearly.
- [ ] Do not talk too loudly or too quietly.
- [ ] Try to convey enthusiasm and interest.
- [ ] Do not use slang or swear words.

Construction of the Olympic Park

A remarkable transformation has taken place in east London, the heart of the London 2012 Games. After the bid was won in 2005, the land to build the Olympic Park was secured and the majority of construction was completed in 2011. As a result, this area of untapped potential has been developed into a spectacular urban park with world-class venues and new infrastructure links.

Planning

The bid was won in 2005 and the Olympic Delivery Authority (ODA) was established in 2006. It was responsible for building the main permanent venues and infrastructure on the Olympic Park, as well as the Olympic Village.

Before formal applications for the new venues were submitted to the planning authority, the ODA carried out extensive consultation with the local community and groups representing themes, such as accessibility, sustainability, security, faith, and health and safety.

Before construction on the 2.5 square kilometre site Olympic Park could begin, the ODA undertook the most extensive and sustainable clean-up operation ever seen in the UK.

The work started as soon as the ODA gained possession of the Olympic Park site in summer 2007. Between then and summer 2008, work focused on preparing the site for construction. The ODA then began constructing the main venues and infrastructure – known as the 'big build'.

The 'big build'

Every year from 2007, the ODA set out what it would achieve each year, to make it accountable for the significant public investment in the construction project.

The final year of the big build saw the construction of all the venues completed – on time and within budget by 27 July 2011 – one year ahead of the Olympic Games Opening Ceremony. They were then handed over to the London 2012 Organising Committee of the Olympic and Paralympic Games (LOCOG) so that they could hold test events and add the finishing touches to transform the facilities into venues ready to stage the Games.

Elsewhere in the country, sporting venues were enhanced or built from scratch, providing world-class facilities for the Games and for the long-term benefit of local communities and elite athletes.

Throughout the construction programme, the aim for the Games was to leave an amazing legacy – for them to be remembered, not only as a summer of fantastic sport, but as the catalyst for the regeneration of one of the most underdeveloped areas of the UK.

In building the venues, we raised the bar for both the construction industry and future large-scale events. In areas as diverse as sustainability, health and safety, equality and inclusion, we set new standards to which others can now aspire.

A Read the text and answer these questions.

1 Where is the Olympic Park?

2 What does ODA stand for?

3 Who did the ODA consult before applying to the planning authority?

4 When did work on the Olympic Park start?

5 What size is the site for the Olympic Park?

6 What did the organising committee do when they took control of the venues?

B Match the dates to what happened in each year.

Date	What happened
2005	Opening Ceremony
2006	Work starts on the site
2007	Olympic Delivery Authority set up
2008	Venues ready
2011	London wins bid for the Games
2012	Preparation of site completed

C The text uses a number of adjectives (words used to describe) to paint a positive picture of the Games. Replace each adjective in brackets with one that has a similar meaning.

1 A (remarkable) [   ] transformation has taken place in east London.

2 An area of untapped potential has been developed into a (spectacular) [   ] urban park.

3 The ODA undertook an (extensive) [   ] clean-up operation.

4 The aim was to leave an (amazing) [   ] legacy.

D The ODA consulted with community groups about issues such as **accessibility**, **sustainability**, **security** and **faith**. Match each of these words to their definition.

Word	Definition
1 Accessibility	a) Protection from loss, attack or harm
2 Sustainability	b) Easy to reach or enter physically and without difficulty
3 Faith	c) Ensuring something can be maintained and natural resources are not destroyed
4 Security	d) A system of religious belief

E The aim for the Games was to 'leave an amazing legacy' that would benefit the UK in the future. In your group, discuss the legacy of the Games.

- According to the text, how did the Games hope to do this?
- Share your thoughts with the rest of the group.
- Do you think that the UK has achieved these benefits?

F Write a paragraph summarising the discussion.

- What points were made? How much did people agree?

Olympic velodrome on list for building of the year prize

The velodrome for the 2012 Olympics, nicknamed 'the giant Pringle' for its crisp-like curves, is in the running to be named building of the year after picking up a design award from the Royal Institute of British Architects (RIBA).

The 6,000-seat building, completed in February, is the first construction at the £9bn Olympic Park in east London to be granted an award by RIBA.

The creators, Hopkins Architects, were advised by Sir Chris Hoy, the multiple gold medal winning track cyclist, and the award looks set to be the first of many for the park.

The velodrome is one of the contenders for the £20,000 Stirling Prize for the architects of the building that has made the greatest contribution to British architecture in the past year. The architects must be RIBA members, but the building can be anywhere in the European Union. However, a lack of design opportunities in the UK has meant that some of British architecture's biggest names have only won prizes for projects in Europe. Last year's Stirling Prize winner, David Chipperfield, won awards for a shopping centre in Innsbruck and a museum in Essen, but nothing for a building in the UK.

G Read the story about the velodrome on page 81 and choose the correct answer to each question.

1 Who is Sir Chris Hoy?

a) An architect ☐

b) A cyclist ☐

c) A builder ☐

2 Last year's winner of the Stirling Prize designed which of these buildings?

a) A museum in Essen ☐

b) A museum in Innsbruck ☐

c) A shopping centre in the UK ☐

3 What does RIBA stand for?

a) Royal International Building Awards ☐

b) Royal Institution of British Architecture ☐

c) Royal Institute of British Architects ☐

4 How much is the Stirling Prize worth?

a) £6,000 ☐

b) £20,000 ☐

c) £9bn ☐

H Write a complete sentence to answer each of these questions.

1 Why is the velodrome nicknamed 'the giant Pringle'?

2 Why has the Stirling Prize been won for projects in Europe but not in the UK?

FOCUS ON Active listening

Some people are described as 'good listeners'. When you think about someone who is good at conversation you may find that it is because they listen more than they speak. Being able to listen attentively and remember what people say is a valuable skill.

A How do you feel if someone you are talking to does the following things?

1 Interrupts you while you are speaking

2 Spends their time leafing through some papers

3 Yawns

4 Keeps looking at their watch

These are all examples of poor listening habits – they make us feel uncomfortable and ill at ease.

B How do you feel if someone you are talking to does the following things?

1 Looks at you kindly

2 Nods their head in agreement

3 Smiles

4 Asks you appropriate questions

5 Makes eye contact

These are examples of good listening habits – they make us feel more comfortable and 'listened to'.

We can all become better listeners by using what is known as 'active listening'. Active listening involves really paying attention to people when they speak, being interested in what they are saying, and showing that you are listening.

 Use this checklist to practise active listening skills.

Active listening checklist

☐ Do not try to do other things when you are meant to be listening.

☐ Sit or stand so that you can see the other person comfortably. Make sure there is enough space to hear each other clearly without crowding them.

☐ Use eye contact well — look at the other person regularly without staring at them.

☐ Use positive body language, such as leaning forward, smiling and other facial expressions.

☐ Avoid things that show lack of interest or impatience, such as folded arms, yawning or tapping your fingers.

☐ Give the speaker time to think and organise their thoughts.

☐ Do not interrupt.

☐ Nod your head. Encourage with comments such as 'Yes' and 'I see'.

☐ Check your understanding of what the person has said from time to time. Say, 'So you mean ...?'

☐ Ask questions to show interest and to encourage the other person to continue.

☐ Make an effort to really *hear* what the person is trying to say. Avoid jumping to conclusions or judging people.

Practise using these techniques next time you listen to someone, whether one to one or in a group.

SOURCE A rotten business

Dry rot and its control

Dry rot is a wood-destroying fungus that is found in most parts of the world. Although it affects forest timbers, dry rot is best known for its ability to destroy timbers in buildings.

It is important to identify whether timber decay has been caused by dry rot or another wood-destroying fungus, such as one of the wet rots. This is because dry rot has the ability to travel through materials other than timber, and so can spread quickly through a building. As the fungus takes a stronger hold on the infected surface, strands called mycelia will spread to infect more wood and provide water for the growth and spread of dry rot.

Typical indications of dry rot

- Active decay produces a musty, damp odour.
- Wood shrinks and darkens and cube-like cracks appear.
- Under less-humid conditions, a silky grey or mushroom-coloured skin, perhaps tinged with patches of lilac and yellow, often develops.
- Under humid conditions white, fluffy 'cottonwool' mycelium develops.
- Strands develop in the mycelium; these are brittle when dry and crack when bent.
- Fruiting bodies are a soft, fleshy pancake or bracket with an orange surface.
- The edges of the fruiting bodies are often dotted with red spores.

Dry rot control and treatment

Dry rot will only affect timber that is damp. Timber can become damp for a number of reasons. Common causes are leaking washing machines, shower trays, baths and condensation. The dampness can also come from outside the building, for example leaking roofs, rising damp or damp penetrating through walls.

Dry rot cannot sustain itself on timber that has less than 20 per cent moisture content. So the first control measure for any dry rot outbreak is to identify the cause of excessive moisture, eliminate it and allow damp areas to dry out quickly in well-ventilated conditions. Once you have tackled the source of the dampness and allowed the timber to dry out, the dry rot will eventually be controlled.

It is not always possible or practical to be sure that the timbers will remain dry in the long term. Therefore, you may need to take secondary measures to defend against reinfection. Remove any affected timbers and put them in sealed polythene bags. Replace them with pretreated timber. Treat any remaining timbers at risk of being affected by the dry rot with a fungicide. Where the dry rot has passed through the masonry, this should be isolated using physical containment and/or masonry sterilisation.

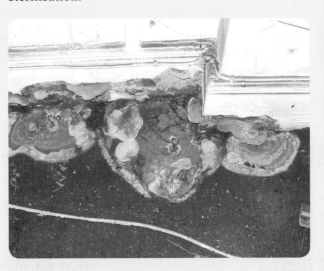

A rotten business

A Read the text and answer these questions.

1 Apart from dry rot, what other kind of fungus might cause timber decay?

2 What is the name for strands of dry rot that spread the infection to more wood?

3 Why is it important to identify the cause of excessive moisture?

4 What sort of smell suggests active timber decay?

5 List three common causes of excessive moisture from within the home.

a)

b)

c)

6 What is the purpose of secondary measures to control dry rot?

B Insert a word from the list below in each gap.

condensation   spread   control   fungus   suspected   edges   smell   pancake

I first [ ] that we might have dry rot in our house when there was a musty [ ] in the shower room. The extractor fan had not worked for a while so there was a lot of [ ]. Later [ ] started to appear. It was shaped like a [ ] and was orange with red [ ]. I called my builder, who managed to [ ] it before it [ ] to other parts of the house.

C Put these steps for dealing with dry rot in the correct order by numbering each point.

- Treat remaining timber that is at risk with a fungicide. ☐
- Place timber in sealed bags. ☐
- Replace with pretreated timber. ☐
- Ventilate the area. ☐
- Remove affected timber. ☐

D Which of these statements is true and which is false, according to the article?

1 Dry rot only spreads through wood. True ☐ False ☐

2 Dry rot cannot live in timber with a moisture content of less than 20 per cent. True ☐ False ☐

3 Wet rot also destroys wood. True ☐ False ☐

4 Dry rot is caused by bacteria. True ☐ False ☐

E Match each word to its definition.

Word	Definition
1 Humid	a) An organism that reproduces by way of spores
2 Ventilate	b) A high level of moisture in the air
3 Fungus	c) To put something right
4 Rectify	d) To provide fresh air in an enclosed space

F Choose two of the words in Activity E and write each of them in a separate sentence.

1

2

G Imagine that you have been called to a house because there is a damp problem in the kitchen. You can see that there has been an outbreak of dry rot, caused by a leaking washing machine. It has spread through the masonry.

• Work in pairs, with one of you taking the role of the homeowner and the other the role of the builder.

• The builder has to explain to the homeowner what the problem is and how they will deal with it. The homeowner says that they just want the builder to get rid of the damp and put on a new coat of paint.

H The article about dry rot is roughly 400 words long. Summarise it so that it is 100 words long or less.

• Go through the article and identify the main points by underlining them or using a highlighter pen.

• Cross out any unnecessary information.

Your summary should cover:

• what dry rot is

• the damage it does

• how to spot dry rot

• how to deal with dry rot.

I List three measures that you could take to protect yourself when using a fungicide.

1

2

3

Hazardous substances

People working in construction may be exposed to substances that could harm their health. The term for these is 'hazardous substances'.

The Control of Substances Hazardous to Health Regulations (COSHH) 2002 are there to protect workers' health in all industries. Employers have to:

- assess the risks of working with the hazardous substances
- eliminate or reduce these risks
- introduce measures to control the risks where it is not possible to eliminate them
- monitor the health of employees where necessary.

If a COSHH risk assessment has been made everyone has to follow it.

What are the risks?

Examples of hazardous substances used in construction include:

- concrete/mortar – the lime found in these materials is particularly hazardous, as is the dust created when these substances are handled and mixed
- dust – wood dust is created by cutting, grinding, sanding, etc.
- cleaning agents – such as descalers and acid solutions used to clean bricks
- decorating materials – such as paints, varnishes and paint stripper.
- LEV – local exhaust ventilation.

Construction workers also need to be aware of Weil's disease – a bacterial infection spread by rats. It is found in water and moist soil, both of which are common on building sites.

The risk assessment

To carry out COSHH risk assessments, employers should think about how each substance is used and for what tasks. They should pay particular attention to any processes that produce dust, vapour, fumes or gas that people could breathe in. They should also look out for substances that come into contact with the skin such as dusts or liquids.

Employers need to consider whether substances are used in conditions that could increase the risk, such as extreme weather, or in restricted spaces. They can then decide on the action they need to take to prevent or control exposure to hazardous substances. They should start with the substances that could cause most harm. The results of the assessment must be shared with employees.

A In a group, discuss these questions.

- Have you heard of COSHH?

- Do you know a company that does COSHH risk assessments?

- Who should write the risk assessment?

- What training have you had about hazardous substances?

B Match the words with their meanings.

Word		Meaning	
1	Hazardous	a)	Agent of disease
2	Lime	b)	Can harm living things or the environment
3	Eliminate	c)	The chemical calcium oxide
4	Infection	d)	To get rid of something

C Write down some of the hazardous substances you might come across in your trade/ on site. Consider what the risks of the substances are and how to eliminate or control them.

Compare your list with others in your group.

D Read the statements and write the answers in the grid.

1 A word to describe something that could be dangerous to health.

2 A disease spread by rats.

3 Initials for the regulations to control hazardous substances.

4 Acid solutions may be used to clean these.

5 A risk created by cutting, sanding, and so on.

1					r		
2					i		
3					s		
4					k		
5					s		

E Choose two of the words from the grid above and write them each in a separate sentence.

1

2

F With a partner, make a list of ways in which an organisation you know reduces the risks from hazardous substances.

G What would you say?

An important part of any group discussion is responding to what other people say. If someone said the following things to you about protecting health in the workplace, what would you say?

- You cannot just reply 'I agree' or 'I disagree'.
- You need to add something more to the discussion.

1 'It takes too long to do the COSHH paperwork. I just do not have the time.'

What would you say?

2 'Builders are able to look after themselves. They do not need a nanny state telling them how to stay healthy.'

What would you say?

3 'All construction employers are as bad as each other. None of them care about their workers' health and safety.'

What would you say?

4 'Building workers should take more care of their own health and safety, not leave it all to management.'

What would you say?

FOCUS ON Quote marks

We use quote marks (also called 'speech marks') when we want
to include words that somebody has said, as in these examples:

- 'What time will we meet?' asked Tom.

- Ruth replied, '7.30 would be good.'

- Tom said, 'That's great. See you then.'

The quote marks show which words are spoken, in much the same way as speech bubbles in a cartoon.

Note that if you start a sentence with someone 'said' or similar, you should put a comma before the quote.

When you should use quote marks:

- Every time a new person speaks, start a new paragraph.

- Put quote marks at the start and at the end of the spoken text.

- Use either single (') or double (") quote marks, but be consistent.

- Start each quote with a capital letter.

- Include punctuation (like the question mark above) within the quote marks.

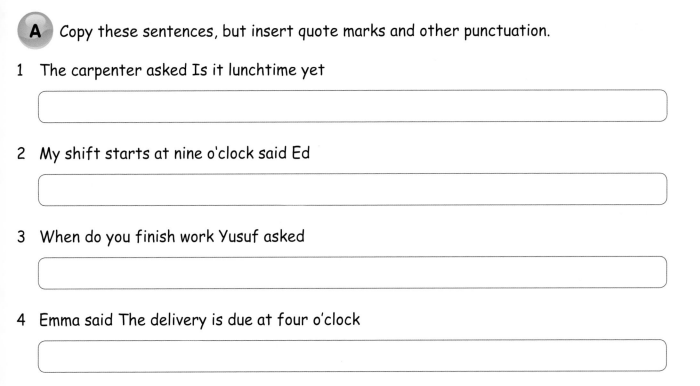

A Copy these sentences, but insert quote marks and other punctuation.

1 The carpenter asked Is it lunchtime yet

2 My shift starts at nine o'clock said Ed

3 When do you finish work Yusuf asked

4 Emma said The delivery is due at four o'clock

If you have a piece of speech that is split into two parts, the punctuation is different. For example:

- 'That's great,' said Tom. 'See you then.'

Notice that:

- there are two sets of speech marks
- there is a comma at the end of the first piece of speech
- there is a full stop at the end of the second piece of speech.

B Copy these sentences, but insert quote marks and other punctuation.

1 The plaster will take a while to dry said Priya You should be able to start painting after around seven days

2 Shall we have a look at the fuse box asked Jess It might help us to identify the problem

Inverted commas

Just as we use quote marks (or 'inverted commas') to show words that someone has spoken, we can also use them to show:

- the title of a book or article
- an extract from a book, article or the internet that you have included in your writing.

You can include short extracts within a paragraph, with inverted commas before and after each title or extract.

> In the article 'Dermatitis in the construction industry' the writer argues that 'dermatitis can be caused by many things, including wet cement, solvents, dusts, oils, greases and cleaning agents'. They point out that while some skin conditions 'can occur quickly after contact with a strong irritant', if someone becomes allergic to a substance 'this may become permanent'.

Longer extracts may need their own paragraph.

C Try putting quote marks and other punctuation in this paragraph. Use your judgement to decide where quotations might start and finish.

The article Keeping safe on roofs points out that All work on roofs is highly dangerous, even if a job only takes a few minutes. It goes on to argue that Building firms must take proper precautions to control the risk and train their workers about these precautions. One way they can do this is through using a method statement.

Opportunities to work abroad

There is always construction going on in virtually every part of the world. While some countries have been negatively affected by the economic climate, many still have an active construction market.

Employers hiring workers for hands-on, labour-intensive jobs in construction abroad tend to look for experience over qualifications. The more experience you have, the greater the choice and availability of work. Voluntary sector projects, such as building dams or water and sewage infrastructure, also require construction workers.

While there are no European-wide construction qualifications, UK qualifications and institutional membership or chartered status are widely accepted and respected by construction organisations in most parts of the world.

As a national of a country in the European Union (EU), you have the right to work in any of the other 26 member states, such as Poland or Germany. You do not need a work permit. You will also have the same rights as nationals of that country in terms of working conditions, pay and social security. If you are looking for construction work in a country outside the EU you may need to apply for a working visa.

The CSCS card

In the UK, many employers require workers to carry the Construction Skills Certification Scheme (CSCS) card. The CSCS card that you qualify for depends on your level of training, experience and qualifications.

For most cards you have to pass the Construction Skills Health and Safety Test. This is a multiple-choice exam of 50 questions, which lasts 45 minutes.

There are several different types of card.

Red card – trainee (Craft and Operative). Available if you are a trainee and registered for an NVQ or SVQ (or Construction Award), but have not yet achieved Level 2 or 3.

Red card – trainee (Technical, Supervisory and Management). Available if you can provide evidence of current registration with a further/higher education college or university for a nationally recognised construction qualification.

Green card – The green card is available to operatives who carry out basic site skills only (e.g. labourers). There are two ways to apply for a green card: via NVQ or SVQ Level 1, or by employer's recommendation using the industry accreditation competencies.

Blue card – skilled worker. Available if you have achieved an NVQ or SVQ Level 2 or completed an employer-sponsored apprenticeship that included the achievement of a C&G Craft Certificate.

Gold card – skilled worker. Available if you have achieved an NVQ or SVQ Level 3, or if you have completed an approved indentured apprenticeship or an employer sponsored apprenticeship that included the achievement of a C&G Advanced Craft Certificate.

A Read the text about working abroad and answer the questions.

1 What do employers look for when hiring workers for labour-intensive jobs?

2 What might you need to apply for if you are looking for a job outside the EU?

3 What type of CSCS card should you apply for if you are a trainee?

4 What exam might you need to take to qualify for a CSCS card?

5 What Level NVQ/SVQ do you need to have achieved in order to get a gold card?

6 Give two examples of a voluntary sector construction project.

B Which of these statements are true and which are false, according to the text?

1 You need a permit to work in Germany. True ☐ False ☐

2 The CSCS card is recognised in some EU countries. True ☐ False ☐

3 It is compulsory to hold a CSCS card to work in the UK. True ☐ False ☐

4 You can get a green CSCS card even if you have no formal qualifications. True ☐ False ☐

5 If you get a job in an EU country you are likely to be paid less than people from that country. True ☐ False ☐

C Discuss the following points with a partner.

1 Would you ever consider working abroad?

2 What are the reasons for your answer?

3 What benefits could there be from spending a period of time working overseas?

4   Where would you prefer to work – which countries would you be interested in?

In this box, write your name at the top of the left-hand column and your partner's name at the top of the other column. Make notes about how you both responded to each question.

1	1
2	2
3	3
4	4

D   Match the two parts of each sentence.

Part 1
1   The construction industry in some countries
2   UK qualifications, such as NVQs,
3   The CSCS card
4   If you are studying for a degree in construction

Part 2
a)   are respected by construction companies in other EU countries.
b)   you can apply for a red CSCS card.
c)   has been negatively affected by the economic crisis.
d)   that you qualify for depends on your level of training, experience and qualifications.

E   Replace the two words in brackets with a contraction using an apostrophe.

For example:

(I am) [   ] going to apply for a CSCS card.

I'm going to apply for a CSCS card.

1   Now that (I have) [   ] passed my NVQ Level 3, I might look for work in France.

2   If you were working for a company in Holland, (you would) [   ] have the same rights as the Dutch employees.

3   I'm thinking of looking for work in Canada, so (I shall) [   ] have to find out if I need a visa.

4   Qualifications are important but (it is) [   ] also important to have experience.

Liam's story

I answered an advertisement in a trade magazine offering jobs in construction in the Middle East. The agency promised me high wages and said that UK workers were valued and treated well. I had to pay a fee of £300 for them to make the arrangements and do the administration. I was offered a job as a tile setter with a company building a golf resort. From what they said, I thought that the company would pay my airfare, but I found I had to pay it myself. That was another £240.

When I got to the site and found the office, they took ages to find my details. Eventually I was taken to my accommodation – if you could call it that. I had to share a room with three other men, one from the UK and two from India. It was cramped and filthy and we had one gas ring to cook on. After the cost of this was taken from my wages, I found that I was only getting £330 a month. I'd been promised at least £2,000. You don't have the same rights as in the UK – there are no unions and my contract wasn't worth the paper it was written on. In the end, I had to borrow money from my parents to get a flight home.

F Read Liam's story above and answer these questions. Write each answer as a full sentence.

1 How did Liam find out about the job?

2 What job was Liam employed to do?

3 What did Liam have to pay for before he even started working?

4 What was Liam's accommodation like?

5 How did Liam get home?

G As a group, discuss what Liam could have done to avoid these problems.

H Using the ideas from the discussion, write a checklist of what people should find out and do if they are thinking about working abroad in a non-EU country.

Working time and the minimum wage

If you are under 18 but over school-leaving age you are classed as a young worker. You reach school-leaving age at the end of the summer term of the school year in which you turn 16.

Working time limits

A young worker cannot usually be made to work more than eight hours per day or 40 hours per week. These hours cannot be averaged over a longer period and you are not allowed to ignore these restrictions.

You'll only be able to work longer hours if you need to:

- keep the continuity of service or production, or
- respond to a surge in demand for a service or product.

This is provided that:

- there is no adult available to do the work, and
- your training needs are not negatively affected.

The minimum wage

You become eligible for the national minimum wage (NMW) when you're older than school-leaving age. The rate of NMW will then depend on your exact age. There isn't a NMW for people under 16.

There are different levels of NMW, depending on your age and whether you are an apprentice. The rates from 1 October 2012 are:

- £6.19 per hour – the main rate for workers aged 21 and over
- £4.98 per hour – the 18–20 rate
- £3.68 per hour – the 16–17 rate for workers above school-leaving age but under 18.

The apprentice rate is £2.65 per hour for apprentices under 19, or for those aged 19 or over and in the first year of their apprenticeship.

Most workers in the UK over school-leaving age are legally entitled to be paid at least the NMW and all employers have to pay it to you if you are entitled to it. It makes no difference:

- if you are paid weekly or monthly, by cheque, in cash or in another way
- if you work full time, part time or any other working pattern
- if you work at your employer's own premises or on site
- what size your employer is
- where you work in the UK.

You are entitled to the NMW even if you sign a contract agreeing to be paid at a lower rate. This is regardless of whether you sign of your own free will or because your employer persuades or makes you – you must still be paid the proper rate.

The Pay and Work Rights Helpline gives confidential help and advice on the NMW. If you need to work longer than 40 hours a week or you think your employer is unfairly asking you to work over this limit, you can call them on 0800 917 2368. The helpline can take calls in over 100 languages.

A Read the text and answer the questions.

1 What does NMW stand for?

2 What is the NMW for people aged 18–20?

3 Who can you call for help and advice about the NMW?

4 What is the maximum time each day that a young worker can usually be made to work for?

5 In what circumstances can a young worker be asked to exceed the working time limit?

6 When does a young person reach school-leaving age?

B Which of these statements are true and which are false?

1 The Pay and Work Rights Helpline will tell your employer that you contacted them. True ☐ False ☐

2 A young worker cannot normally be made to work more than 40 hours a week. True ☐ False ☐

3 The NMW does not apply to you if you are paid in cash. True ☐ False ☐

4 An apprentice aged 25 and in their first year is entitled to a NMW of £2.65 per hour. True ☐ False ☐

5 A young worker will be under 18 years old. True ☐ False ☐

6 All workers above school-leaving age in the UK are entitled to a NMW of at least £4.98 per hour. True ☐ False ☐

C Insert a word from the list below into the text so that it makes sense.

hour   jobs   minimum   increase   opposed

The national [ ] wage was introduced in the UK in 1999 when it

was set at £3.60 per [ ]. People who [ ]

the NMW said that it would reduce the number of [ ] and

[ ] inflation, but that did not happen.

D Write a sentence to answer each of the following questions. Make sure you use capital letters and full stops where they are needed.

1 Do small employers have to pay the NMW?

2 I am from Romania and my English is not very good. Will the helpline understand me?

3 My employer made me sign a contract to be paid £2.50 an hour. Does that mean I am not entitled to the NMW?

E Read about the person below.

I am an apprentice on a building site. A lot of the other people there work a 50- or 60-hour week. My manager says I must do the same as it's normal in our sector. I'm only given the rubbish jobs to do such as clearing up and making coffee – I'm not learning anything. I also miss my off-job training days sometimes. It's making me really tired and I'm struggling to complete my portfolio.

What advice would you give this person?

F Discuss wages and working hours in your group.

- Do staff in construction work long hours?
- Do you think that workers in construction are well paid?
- Why do people choose to work in construction?
- What do you know about trade unions? How do they help? Would you join one?

G Choose the correct answer to these questions.

1 The NMW for workers over 21 is:

   a) £4.98 ☐

   b) £6.19 ☐

   c) £3.68 ☐

2 The NMW does not apply to:

   a) people paid a monthly salary ☐

   b) people under 16 ☐

   c) people who agree to a lower rate ☐

3 The Pay and Work Rights Helpline give advice on:

   a) contracts of employment ☐

   b) health and safety at work ☐

   c) working time limits ☐

H Draft a leaflet for apprentices aged 16–19 telling them about their rights.

FOCUS ON **Preparing a talk**

You may be asked to give a talk or presentation, either as part of your course or at work. To do this well, you need to consider four key elements:

* planning
* using visual aids
* rehearsing or practising
* getting feedback.

Planning

Start by identifying a topic or subject for your presentation and then think about the purpose and audience.

* Purpose: is your presentation intended to *inform*, *persuade* or *advise*?

* Audience: what do they *already* know. What *language* and *style* is appropriate?

A presentation must have a clear structure. It should start with a general introduction telling people what the talk is about and end with a summary of what you have said.

You should then identify the main sections. For a 10-minute presentation you should have three to five main headings organised in a logical order.

A Here are the main headings for a talk about how a construction organisation handles complaints. Organise them into a logical sequence. Number them from 1 to 6.

☐ Examples of complaints
☐ Summary
☐ Listening to a complaint
☐ Company or organisation procedures
☐ Introduction
☐ How complaints are resolved

Once you have identified your main headings, you can add details of what you will say under each one.

For example, under 'Listening to a complaint' your plan may include the following points:

* Be respectful and courteous.
* Find somewhere private to talk so that you can maintain confidentiality.
* Listen carefully to the individual and be aware of your body language.
* Keep calm and speak quietly to help the person relax.
* Acknowledge the complaint so that they know they have been heard.
* Do not prejudge the situation or offer your own opinion.
* Tell the person what will happen next.

B How will you plan the outline of your talk? Tick the one that suits you best.

☐ Write down all of your ideas on the topic and then organise them in order.

☐ Use a mind map to organise your ideas.

☐ Write a list and then reorganise it.

☐ Use a storyboard format similar to that used for a film or video.

Using visual aids

Relevant images and visual aids can really bring a presentation to life. They can include:

- images, such as photographs, diagrams and paintings
- a model or other physical object or a wall display
- PowerPoint, whiteboard or flipchart.

If you use PowerPoint you can incorporate diagrams and pictures. Be careful not to put too many words on a slide or people will be reading it rather than listening to you.

Cue cards

Cue cards will help you when you are giving your presentation. They:

- are easy to hold and avoid long pages of notes
- remind you of your main points through key words or phrases
- will not distract your audience as much as big sheets of paper.

Here are some tips for writing cue cards:

- Use cards about the size of a filing card (15 cm × 10 cm).
- Write one key word or phrase for the main heading.
- Write no more than four more detailed points and number them.
- Write in large letters or capitals.
- Number your cards in case you drop them!

Practising

It is very important to practise your presentation before you do it for real. Think of it as a rehearsal for a performance. This will help both with the content and with aspects of delivery such as tone of voice and speed.

Decide whether you will practise on your own in front of a mirror or by recording yourself, with a friend, with your tutor or in front of a small group.

If you do practise in front of others, it is worthwhile to ask them for feedback to help understand your strengths and weaknesses.

 **Cowboy builders**

Shoddy work of jailed cowboy builder

The shoddy work of a cowboy builder was exposed on the Channel Five programme 'Cowboy Builders' after he tricked homeowners into handing over 90 per cent of the payment up front – and then left before the job was done.

John Guerin, 56, left dozens of homes across London in a 'state of ruin' and in need of emergency structural repairs over a five-year period in a £370,000 rip-off.

Many of the homes he targeted were left with gaping holes in walls or with full skips in the driveway which had not been paid for. Others had to be rewired or re-plumbed because the work was unsafe. At one property Guerin left the roof uncovered after the old one had been stripped away.

In another instance, foundations were laid for an extension and the first few layers of bricks were laid before the con man fled.

Some were left in such a dangerous condition that they were in peril of collapsing and homeowners had to stump up tens of thousands to get professional builders in to complete the job before they could move back in. Many owners had to remortgage their homes in order to pay for builders to come in and fix Guerin's shoddy work.

John Guerin was jailed for five years at Croydon Crown Court after being found guilty of 10 charges of fraud and one of obtaining money by deception.

The con man targeted vulnerable people and, after starting work, convinced customers to hand over as much cash as possible before he vanished.

In total, cowboy builders rip off homeowners by a staggering £260m a year, a study has revealed. According to research done by the Federation of Master Builders (FMB), people who pay builders in cash lose the equivalent of £712,000 a day in shoddy work, which then has to be repaired.

A spokesman for the FMB, the largest trade association in the UK building industry with a membership of 12,000 building firms, said that paying for work in cash was 'dangerous'.

The research by the FMB showed that, of the 1,000 people quizzed in the poll, 11 per cent said they had ended up with shoddy workmanship, which they then needed to get redone. Of that 11 per cent, 76 per cent had paid in cash – showing that using cash to pay builders was more likely to lead to poor-quality work.

Brian Berry, spokesperson for the FMB, said today: 'Before employing a builder, it is vital to carry out checks to make sure you are using someone reputable, such as an FMB builder. Choosing your builder on price alone can be a false economy which may neither add value to your property nor make for a smooth building project.'

A Read the text and answer these questions.

1 How was the poor-quality work uncovered?

2 How long had it been going on?

3 What did homeowners have to do to put things right?

4 Who carried out research into cowboy builders?

5 What happened to the builder after he was prosecuted?

6 What is paying in cash more likely to lead to?

7 What is the FMB? What do the initials stand for?

B Find three examples of the shoddy workmanship that are given in the article.

1

2

3

C Which of these statements are true and which are false, according to the article?

1 The FMB carried out research with 1,000 people. True ☐ False ☐

2 Around 76 per cent of the people in the FMB research had ended up with shoddy workmanship. True ☐ False ☐

3 John Guerin was charged with endangering life. True ☐ False ☐

4 Some of the owners had to remortgage their homes. True ☐ False ☐

D Why do you think a homeowner might agree to pay a builder money up front or in cash? Write down as many reasons as you can think of.

E The article says that 'Choosing your builder on price alone can be a false economy.'

1 What is meant by the term 'a false economy'?

2 Which of these is a false economy, a) or b)? Circle the correct answer.

 a) Buying a cheap car with no warranty that goes wrong in the first week and costs hundreds of pounds to put right.

 b) Buying a cheap car that you know is faulty and spending time and money doing it up as a hobby so that it runs perfectly.

3 Which of these is a false economy, a) or b)? Circle the correct answer.

 a) Buying a 'buy one get one free' chicken from the supermarket and giving the spare one to a friend.

 b) Buying two chickens from the supermarket that are part of a 'buy one get one half price' offer, but one of them goes off and you have to throw it away.

4 Think of another example of a false economy and write it below.

F As a group, share your examples of false economies. Does anyone have experience of making a false economy?

G Choose a word from the list below to fill each gap.

inspected   credit   find   advice   Code   reputation   website   Master

Before you choose a builder you should check that they have a good

[_____]. One way is to ask them if they are a member of the

Federation of [_____] Builders. FMB members will have passed

[_____] checks and have had their work [_____]. They

also have to sign up to the FMB [_____] of Practice. There is a lot of

[_____] and information on their [_____] www.fmb.org.uk

and you can also use it to [_____] builders in your area.

Tighter checks to keep cowboy builders out

New measures have been put in place to help protect people from cowboy builders. Tradespeople who operate under self-check schemes, which allow them to check their own work, will be required to meet higher standards and prove they meet the right levels of quality, giving householders the peace of mind that work on their homes is up to scratch.

Around 85,000 complaints are made about building work in homes each year according to the Office of Fair Trading.

Communities Minister Andrew Stunell said: 'Cowboy builders give the rest of the industry a bad name. I'm determined to ensure that consumers are properly protected. By raising the bar even higher for self-check tradespeople, we are sorting the rogues from the professionals, making it easier for people to identify competent installers and giving them the confidence that they will receive a high quality of work – or be protected if they don't.'

H Read the text above and choose the correct answer to each question.

1 Under a self-check scheme, who checks the quality of a builder's work?
   a) The builder who carried out the work ☐
   b) The home owner ☐
   c) The Office of Fair Trading ☐

2 Who estimates that 85,000 complaints are made about building work in homes every year?
   a) The Federation of Master Builders ☐
   b) The Office of Fair Trading ☐
   c) The Home Office ☐

3 Who said that 'Cowboy builders give the rest of the industry a bad name'?
   a) Channel Five ☐
   b) Communities Minister Andrew Stunell ☐
   c) A tabloid newspaper ☐

I Tick whether the statements below are fact or opinion.

		Fact	Opinion
1	Cowboy builders give the industry as a whole a bad name.		
2	New measures have been put in place to protect people from cowboy builders.		
3	The FMB is the largest trade association in the UK building industry.		
4	The improvements to the self-check system will give people peace of mind.		
5	Paying builders in cash leads to poor-quality work.		
6	Eleven per cent of the people in the survey said that they ended up with poor workmanship.		

J Work in pairs or groups of three. Think about tips and advice that could help people to choose a reliable, honest and competent builder. Write them as a checklist.

SOURCE Keep it green!

Green-belt land and its purpose

Green-belt land is an area that is kept as open space, usually around larger cities. The main purpose of green-belt policy is to protect the land around larger towns and cities from urban sprawl, and maintain the area for forestry and agriculture as well as to provide habitats for wildlife.

Green-belt land offers a number of benefits for both the urban and rural population. It helps to protect agricultural activities and the unique character of rural communities. It gives the urban population an open space which offers opportunities for outdoor activities and access to clean air.

Currently, green-belt land covers about 13 per cent of the total area in England, 16 per cent in Northern Ireland and 2 per cent in Scotland. Wales has only one green-belt area, which is located between Newport and Cardiff.

Areas that are designated as green belt must not be built upon because green belt is defined as an open space. However, buildings for agricultural uses are usually allowed. In some cases, it is also possible to change the use of land in the green belt and even gain permission for structures that are officially not allowed in a green belt.

Green-belt policy has been shown to have a number of positive effects. It has helped to protect rural communities, historic towns, the natural environment and landscape by the strict restriction of building activities within the designated areas. It has also improved quality of air in urban centres and provided recreational opportunities in the natural and semi-natural environment for people who live in cities.

A disadvantage of green-belt policy is that it creates a physical barrier that prevents the normal expansion of towns and cities. The number of people working and living in urban centres is likely to continue to increase and, without increased building activity, it will be difficult for future generations to find their own home. The building restrictions are also an obstacle to the expansion of industries and businesses.

Critics of green-belt policy have also pointed out that some areas are of poor quality or are poorly managed, providing little or no benefit to the nearby population and the environment.

A Each of the words below has a similar meaning to one in the table. Write the words in the right place in the table.

distinctive   city   selected   spread

1	urban	
2	sprawl	
3	unique	
4	designated	

B Read the text and answer these questions.

1 What is the main purpose of green-belt policy?

2 What is restricted on green-belt land?

3 Which country in the UK has the largest percentage of green-belt land?

4 What kind of buildings are usually allowed on green-belt land?

5 How do people who live in towns benefit from green-belt land?

6 What industries can operate on green-belt land?

C The text explains some of the advantages and disadvantages of green-belt policy. Write them in the box below.

Advantages	Disadvantages

D Look at the advantages and disadvantages you have found. Decide whether you support existing green-belt policy or think it should be modified.

Form a group of four including some who think green-belt policy should be kept as it is and others who think it needs to be changed. Share your opinions in a discussion making sure that you:

- make your points clearly
- back them up with facts and examples where possible
- allow everyone to take turns
- listen carefully to what others say
- are prepared to change your mind if a better argument is presented.

E Read the article below. Decide which of the statements are true and which are false.

Hotel ordered to remove unauthorised outdoor drinking area

The Casa Hotel has developed an outside area on what used to be ground that sloped downwards towards the lake and was raised to create a horizontal surface with a retaining wall of gabion baskets.

Calderdale Council has been in dispute about whether the development contravenes Government policy for building on green-belt land. An appeal made by the owner, Jack McDaid, has been rejected by planning inspector Mike Croft.

The inspector said the building did not integrate with the surrounding green-belt land. He also had doubts about the safety of the development, saying. 'I saw for myself that the wall appears to be bulging at several points at its lower levels where it is touching the Water Ski Club's palisade fence. That is supported by concerns about possible pollution that arise from the absence of information about the nature of the material backfilled behind the wall.' He concluded that the total harm clearly outweighed the benefits.

Mr McDaid argued that the development does not need to be removed entirely to satisfy green-belt policy, and that the extent of the raised and levelled area and the gabion baskets could be reduced, with mitigating landscaping.

The Casa has also been ordered to demolish a building measuring 6.2 m by 4.6 m and used for storage, as it is also inappropriate in terms of green-belt policy.

Which of these statements are true and which are false, according to the article?

1	The hotel owner's appeal was successful.	True ☐	False ☐
2	The planning inspector thought the development was unsafe.	True ☐	False ☐
3	Some of the material used might cause pollution.	True ☐	False ☐
4	The hotel owner did not have planning permission.	True ☐	False ☐
5	The outdoor drinking area was attractive.	True ☐	False ☐
6	The hotel is near a lake.	True ☐	False ☐

F Choose a word from the ones below to fill the gap in each sentence.

quality   demolish   wildlife   planning

1   If you want to put up a new building you must apply for _____ permission.

2   If you do not have permission, the local council can order you to _____ a building.

3   The green-belt policy has improved the _____ of air in towns.

4   The green belt protects _____ and the environment.

G Recent government policy allows local councils to take more land out of green belt. Draft an email to your local newspaper saying why you think this is a good or bad idea.

FOCUS ON Writing good paragraphs

Paragraphs are important in all pieces of writing that are more than a few sentences long. They provide a clear structure to longer emails, letters, assignments and reports. Good paragraphs divide up the text and separate out the main ideas. They make it easier for the reader to follow your argument.

The principles for writing good paragraphs are as follows:

- Use a new paragraph for each new idea.
- A paragraph can have just one or two sentences, though it will usually have three to six sentences.
- Each paragraph begins with the 'topic sentence', which introduces the idea.
- The other sentences then provide more information about this idea.
- All of the sentences should be relevant to the main idea.

Look at the first paragraph on this page. The topic sentence is the one beginning 'Paragraphs are important'. The other sentences explain why they are important. There are four sentences altogether.

A Read the following paragraph. Which is the topic sentence? How many other sentences are there?

There are different types of paragraph. You begin your piece of writing with an introductory paragraph, which introduces what you will write, and why you are writing it. You then have one paragraph for each of the main ideas. You end with a concluding paragraph, which sums up what you have said.

Punctuating paragraphs

You punctuate paragraphs like this:

- Begin a new paragraph with a new line.
- Either leave a line space before the new paragraph, or indent the first line of the paragraph.
- Each sentence begins with a capital letter and ends with a full stop (or a question mark or exclamation mark).

B Turn the information above on punctuating paragraphs into a paragraph rather than a bullet list. You can use the same words, though you may want to make a few minor changes so that the paragraph reads better. Make sure you begin with a good topic sentence.

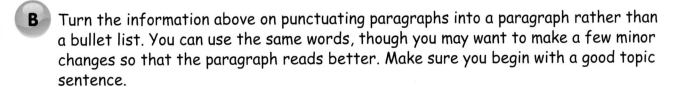

Introducing the paragraph

As we have seen, the first sentence is likely to be the topic sentence and will introduce the idea in the paragraph. Where possible, it is good to link back to what has gone before. You can do this with phrases such as 'as we have seen', 'on the other hand' or 'however'. Try to make the topic sentence as interesting as possible.

Developing the paragraph

The other sentences will develop the idea in the topic sentence. They can do this in several ways such as:

- explaining the idea in greater detail
- providing a list (like this one!)
- giving an example
- including some facts or figures.

However, the sentences must all be relevant to the topic and must never introduce a new idea.

Ending the paragraph

The final sentence may simply round off the paragraph. In some cases it may sum up what you have said or lead in to the next paragraph.

C Turn these words and phrases into a paragraph about the role of a construction worker.

> construction workers   important role   today's society
>
> over 2 million UK construction workers   almost 7 per cent of all jobs
>
> range of trades   must work together   health and safety is vital
>
> more accidents than in other sectors   follow procedures

Write your paragraph on a separate piece of paper.

D Next time you need to draft a paragraph, use this checklist to check what you have written.

- ☐ Does the paragraph start a new line?
- ☐ Is there a clear topic sentence?
- ☐ Do other sentences develop the main idea?
- ☐ Are all sentences relevant to the main idea?
- ☐ Is the paragraph interesting?
- ☐ Is the punctuation correct?

Being self-employed

One of the main attractions of becoming self-employed is no longer having to work for somebody else. But there are some things you should consider before you decide. These include not being certain of having a regular income, having to arrange your own sick pay and pension and probably having to work long hours.

Types of business

There are a number of different types of business that you can set up.

- A sole trader. This is the simplest way of starting a business. It just involves you, working for yourself, with no employees.

- A partnership. This is similar to a sole trader except that two or more people run the business. You may or may not have employees.

- A limited company. This is run by directors and gives the business a completely separate identity from the people who run it. It is more complicated to set up.

Keeping accounts

It is extremely important to keep accurate and detailed records of the business. You will have to keep your own books or employ a bookkeeper or accountant.

Tax and VAT

As a self-employed person, you will be responsible for paying income tax on your earnings and will usually need the help of an accountant to complete your tax return.

Whether or not a self-employed person has to pay VAT depends on the type of business and the turnover of the business. If you register for VAT, in your invoices you will have to add the VAT (20 per cent in 2012) to the cost of labour and materials.

Insurance

The law requires you to take out certain types of insurance. Other types of insurance are not compulsory, but it is important to consider which ones are appropriate.

- Vehicles used for work must be insured for business purposes even if they are already insured for private use.

- Public liability insurance. This provides cover against claims by members of the public who have been injured or had property damaged as a result of carelessness at work by you or your employees.

- If you employ other people you will have to take out employer's liability insurance.

National Insurance and pensions

As a self-employed person you may have to pay National Insurance contributions. The payment of contributions will affect the benefits you can claim in the future.

As a self-employed person you will get state retirement pension if you have made the correct National Insurance contributions. You could also consider taking out a private pension.

Cost Ledger

Accounts Payable
Limited plc

Date	Code	Item Name	Debit	Credit	Balance
2013-05-23	83	Phone support	0.00	120.00	−120.00
2013-07-15	25	Company report	0.00	240.00	−360.00
2013-10-12	19	Restock goods	0.00	600.00	−960.00
		Total	0.00	720.00	−960.00

A Read the text and answer these questions.

1 Who might help a self-employed person with their tax return?

2 Give two ways you could make sure you get a pension.

a)

b)

3 What was the VAT rate in 2012?

4 Write down two disadvantages of being self-employed.

a)

b)

5 What type of insurance protects you if a member of the public is injured as a result of your work?

B Match the example to the type of business.

Example		Type of business
1 Conrad and Frank are decorators. They run their business together, sharing all of the risks and the profits.		a) Limited company
2 Anna works as an interior designer. She works from home and there is no one else involved in her business. She takes on all of the risk and receives all of the profits.		b) Partnership
3 Five people who worked together on a project have decided to set up a business. They will all be directors and will employ other people as well.		c) Sole trader

C Discuss the questions below with a partner. Make notes about your discussion.

- Have you ever considered being self-employed?
- What type of business would you choose?
- Do you know other people who are self-employed?
- What would be the advantages for you?
- What would be the disadvantages?

D Read the information about VAT and choose the correct word to write in each gap.

turnover   expensive   bills   threshold   government
materials   profit   claim   registered   less   employed

Any self-_____ person can register for VAT but it is not compulsory if your turnover is less than £77,000 a year (in 2012). This is called the VAT threshold.

Your _____ is the total amount that the business earns, not just the _____. However, the VAT _____ can be changed by the _____ so it is important to keep up-to-date with the tax regulations. The advantage of being VAT _____ is that you can _____ back the VAT you pay for things you buy for your business, such as _____ or equipment. That means that you actually pay _____ for them. On the other hand, you have to add VAT to the customers' _____ and this might make your quote more _____ than someone else's.

E In the construction industry, it is sometimes hard to tell whether a person is genuinely self-employed. Read the case study below, then answer the questions that follow on page 118.

Employment status

John was a builder who worked with a team of subcontractors on building sites. Usually, he would get a phone call in the morning, pick up the team and take them to the next job. This arrangement gave them the freedom to work when and where they pleased.

They had found a building site near home, and been working there for about six months when John was approached by someone on the site. The man introduced himself as an inspector from HM Revenue and Customs (HMRC). He asked questions about who they were working for, how long they had been there, how they were paid, and whether or not they received holiday or sick pay. The next day, John got a call from his boss at the building company, wanting to know what he had said to the inspector. John answered what he could, and his boss seemed quite concerned.

His boss got in touch with a company called Tax Champion who visited the site, and interviewed him, John and the other subcontractors. HMRC wanted to prove that the subcontractors were all employees, but the tax and National Insurance contributions they would have had to pay would have bankrupted the building company.

They were able to show that none of the subcontractors were employees because there was no 'mutuality of obligation' – one of the three key tests of employment. Mutuality of obligation means that an employer is obliged to provide work for the employee, and the employee is obliged to accept it. The employee can expect regular employment until they are made redundant or leave of their own accord. The company survived, and John was able to carry on choosing when and where he worked.

1   Why did John and the other men like this way of working?

2   Who did the inspector work for?

3   Write down three things the inspector wanted to know.

    a)

    b)

    c)

4   What would have bankrupted the building company?

5   Why were John and his mates not classed as employees?

6   From what you have learnt about self-employment, do you think that John got sick pay from the employer?

F   Complete the two paragraphs below. You can add your own ideas to the ones you have read about in the texts.

The benefits of being an employee are that

The benefits of being self-employed are that

Wimpey and Bovis

The business of building houses has suffered its ups and downs over the years. However, here are two firms that have kept going for a considerable period of time.

Wimpey

This was started by George Wimpey, who was 25 at the time, as a local building company in Hammersmith in 1880. The company built Hammersmith Town Hall in 1896 and laid the foundations for the first electric tramway in London in the late 1890s. The company also built the White City Stadium. Before the First World War, its activities spread into road, tramway and bridge construction.

Taylor Wimpey

George Wimpey died in 1913, aged 58. His family put the business up for sale after the war ended in 1919. It was bought by Godfrey Mitchell who decided to keep the Wimpey name. He developed it into one of the UK's top housebuilding and construction firms and stayed chief executive until 1973.

With the start of the Second World War in 1939, private housebuilding ceased so Wimpey concentrated on defence work, building aerodromes, factories and army camps, and finished the war as one of the country's largest contractors. After the war, building controls made it harder to build private houses so Wimpey turned to building local authority houses. When the controls ended in 1954, Wimpey went back to building private housing and by 1972 it was building more homes than any other contractor. Wimpey Construction also built Heathrow Airport (1946) and participated in the building of the Channel Tunnel (1994).

In 2007 Wimpey merged with another company called Taylor Woodrow and is now Taylor Wimpey. It is still one of the UK's largest housebuilders.

Bovis

In 1885, at the age of 35, Charles William Bovis started a general building company, CW Bovis and Co. He built a number of flats and houses in and around London. One example is a four-storey brick-built residential block in Marylebone, finished in 1893.

In 1908 the company was acquired by Samuel Joseph and his cousin. During the 1920s they constructed buildings for a number of retail clients – Marks and Spencer being the most important and long-lasting. In 1936 The Bovis School of Building opened, with 100 apprentices and management trainees.

BOVIS HOMES

During the war they built a munitions factory and harbours, and after the war the company moved back into the private sector and building houses.

In 1965 Bovis Homes was formed as a separate business, focusing on the private housing market. Bovis Homes expanded and, by 1972, it was the second-largest housebuilder in the UK. It remains one of the UK's most successful housebuilding companies.

A Read the text and answer these questions.

1 Where was George Wimpey's company based when it started?

2 What building did Charles Bovis complete in 1893?

3 What did Wimpey build during the war?

4 Who was an important customer of Bovis in the 1920s?

5 Which company built roads and tramways?

6 Who studied at the Bovis School of Building?

B Put a tick in the box to say whether each fact is true for Wimpey, Bovis or both.

Fact	Wimpey	Bovis	Both
1 Company was started in the 19th century			
2 Built Heathrow Airport			
3 Was the second-largest housebuilder in the UK in 1972			
4 Built a factory during the war			
5 Set up a building school			
6 Had the same chief executive from 1919 to 1973			

C Number these statements to show the correct order in the history of the Wimpey company.

☐ Built the Channel Tunnel

☐ Built houses for local authorities

☐ Sold to Godfrey Mitchell

☐ Built aerodromes and army camps

☐ Became Taylor Wimpey

☐ Built Hammersmith Town Hall

D Read the two texts below and answer the questions that follow.

Buying a new home

At Taylor Wimpey we don't believe that moving house has to be stressful.

You can rely on us. Taylor Wimpey are one of the UK's largest house builders, and with a 10-year National House-Building Council (NHBC) structural warranty, a Taylor Wimpey new home also offers that most valuable added extra, more peace of mind.

You get to choose the personal touches

The beauty of buying with us is choosing for yourself all the crucial details from our styling options range, which turn a house into a home. From door handles to kitchen units, you can choose from a range of high-quality fixtures and finishes, adding those final touches that make a home truly yours.

You buy a home that's part of a growing community

Responsible urban planning is essential to Taylor Wimpey. Whether it's planning our developments around open space or providing safe cycle and pedestrian paths, we create developments that match the lifestyle our customers want to live.

We've even got special offers specifically designed to help you buy one of our fantastic new homes. NewBuy is a new scheme that means you can get a 95 per cent mortgage. It will be available to first-time buyers and existing home owners on all Taylor Wimpey developments across England.

 # Buying for the first time

Buying your own home for the first time is exciting but it can also be daunting. There is a whole new language to learn and everyone will give you advice. **But how do you know who to trust?**

✳✳✳

Welcome to Bovis Homes. We build some of the best new homes in the UK. We create communities and will often use local materials and reflect local features. Trees are retained wherever possible and new landscaping added, along with footpaths and cycleways in many cases to help create a pleasant place to live. We have homes for sale right now that would be ideal for you and we offer you stunning all-inclusive specifications. And we not only build your house. We can help you buy your house. We have put together some of the best home buying assistance schemes on the market – including a 5 per cent deposit mortgage package and a shared equity deal – because we want to get you moving.

✳✳✳

And remember, with <u>so much included as standard</u> in a Bovis Home, you do not need to worry about finding the extra money to buy kitchen appliances and other features such as wardrobes – you'll find many of our homes include these items in the price.

---

1 Tick what you think is the main purpose of the information.

To inform ☐

To persuade ☐

To advise ☐

To reassure ☐

2 How do the companies describe how people feel about buying a house?

3 What does each company say about the environment around the houses they build?

Wimpey say that they

Bovis say that they

4 What do you think are the top three selling points for each company that would persuade people to find out more?

Wimpey	Bovis
1	1
2	2
3	3

Share your top points with the rest of your group to see if they agree.

E Choose a word to fill each gap in the text below.

founders   sector   new   established   sold   original   was   well-known

Wimpey and Bovis are longstanding companies in the housebuilding [   ].

They were both [   ] in the 1880s and are still in business today.

The [   ] of the businesses were quite young – Charles Bovis [   ] 35 and George Wimpey was only 25 when they set them up.

Although the companies had been [   ] to other people before 1920, the [   ] owners kept the [   ] names and Wimpey and Bovis are still [   ] companies.

FOCUS ON Conjunctions and prepositions

You can use conjunctions to join two simple sentences together to make a longer, more interesting sentence. For example:

- 'Mr Andrews would like a chairlift fitted' is a simple sentence.

- 'He has arthritis' is also a simple sentence.

By joining them together with a conjunction we make the sentence:

- 'Mr Andrews would like a chairlift fitted **because** he has arthritis.'

A Choose from the common conjunctions below to join the following sentences together. In most of the cases there will be more than one option.

and   so   but   because   or   though   as

1 I enjoy talking to customers. Some of them can be difficult.

2 It is important to put building waste in that skip. It can be recycled.

3 We organise a site meeting once a week. Different teams can get together and plan the week's work.

4 The chipboard is stored on this shelf. You will find the plywood on this one.

5 I would love to be a surveyor. I do not have the right qualifications.

6 The new brickwork will need covering. It looks like it is going to rain.

B Conjunctions can also contain more than one word. Write a sentence containing one of these conjunctions.

provided that   as long as

Prepositions

You may not know the grammatical term 'preposition', but you will recognise these words and probably know how to use them. A preposition links nouns, pronouns and phrases to other words in a sentence.

C Choose from the prepositions below to fill the gaps in each sentence.

with   about   to   of   for   from

1 The new paint range is very popular [   ] our customers.

2 We were all very sad [   ] Mr Singh's illness.

3 The plaster has dried so it is now ready [   ] paint.

4 I was not aware [   ] the health risks associated [   ] concrete.

5 Now I have been promoted I am responsible [   ] induction [   ] new staff.

6 This building site is completely different [   ] the one I was at before.

7 Off-job training is vital in order [   ] understand the principles of construction work.

D For each of the following phrases, write a sentence that contains the phrase.

pleased with   sorry about   intended for

1

2

3

FOCUS ON **Writing an email**

You may use email to keep in touch with friends or family – these are *informal* emails. Sometimes, however, you will have to write a *formal* email.

Formal emails are anything to do with your professional work, such as an email to a customer or to another person that you have to liaise with in construction. They also include emails relating to job applications or official organisations.

The tips below are very important for formal emails, but many of them apply to informal emails as well.

Top tips for writing effective emails

- Make sure you include something in the subject line. You would be amazed how many people forget to do this. If you are replying to an email you have received it may be all right to keep the subject that is already there, but you need to decide whether you should change it.

- Write a clear and meaningful subject line. People often look at the subject line to decide whether to open or delete a message. Make sure the subject accurately describes the content. Do not put 'Important! Read immediately' or 'Questions'.

- Think about how you will start the email. Although it is more informal than a letter, if you are writing to someone you do not know for the first time, you should still write 'Dear xxx', not 'Hi'.

- Keep your message focused and readable. If you are making a number of points, separate them with bullets, dashes or paragraphs.

- Use standard spelling and avoid shortening words as you might in a text message.

- Only use capitals where you should for correct grammar. Writing all in capitals can come across as SHOUTING!

- Even if you are complaining or angry about something, be polite. Harsh words can sound much ruder in an email.

- If you are writing to someone you do not know, include your full name and any other information they may need, such as a contact telephone number.

- Think about how you will end your email. In a formal letter you might write 'Yours sincerely' or 'Yours faithfully', but it has become common practice in email to end politely with 'Best regards' or 'Kind regards'.

- Read your email carefully before you send it. First read it to see how it sounds — is the tone of voice right?

- Proofread your email for spelling mistakes or typos. Email may be a fast form of communication but that does not mean it should be rushed.

A Look at the email below.

Can you spot any mistakes? How could it be improved?

From: JanetJ@thecarpenters.co.uk	
Subject: Problem	
Date: 22 August 2012 10:31:45	
To: info@timbersupplies.co.uk	

We are not happy with the boards you sent us. Their too thin and our carpenters keep havng accidents. Which makes them very distressed. Weve been using your company for ages and haven't had any problems before so why are we having them now? Are you using cheaper materail or a different supplier. What are you going to do about it.

From

Janet Jones

B Can you think of times when you have had to write a formal email?

Share your examples in the group.

C Draft an email in reply to this job advert. Use the checklist of tips to help you and check your draft when you have finished.

Vacancy for heating engineer assistant

We are looking for a fully qualified engineer with a strong technical knowledge and background. Experience of Golworm boilers would be useful but not essential. Qualifications and full UK driving licence essential. For further details and to apply please email Jill West at jwest@northgarages.co.uk

From:	
Subject:	
Date:	
To:	

FOCUS ON Writing a formal letter

Formal letters include letters that you write in your work, letters for job applications, letters of complaint, and so on. When you write formal letters you should include these required elements:

- Your own address, or the name, address and phone number of your organisation, go at the top of the letter. Many organisations use headed notepaper so there is no need to type in the address.

- The name and address of the person you are writing to go next, on the left-hand side of the page, followed by the date.

- The 'salutation' comes next, which can be Dear Sir/Madam, Dear Mr/Mrs [surname] or Dear [first name] if you know the person well.

- It is then common to include the subject of the letter, or a reference (e.g. 'Re your letter of 5 May 2012').

- You then write the letter, broken into paragraphs.

- If you greeted the recipient by name, you should finish the letter with 'Yours sincerely' followed by your signature and name. If you began with 'Dear Sir/Madam', you should end with 'Yours faithfully'.

For example:

Northern Plumbing
Park Crescent
Manchester M23 4LS
Phone: 0161 123 4567

Mr Ben Simmons
Plumbing Supplies
25 Hincham Lane
Manchester M23 1LB

16 May 2012

Dear Mr Simmons

Plumbing Supplies

I am writing to express our thanks for supplying us with heating controls at short notice. These helped us to meet our customers' needs during the recent bad weather.

We would like to set up a preferred supplier arrangement with your company and I would be grateful if you could let me know the terms on which this could be arranged.

I look forward to hearing from you.

Yours sincerely

David Lawton

David Lawton, Service Manager

A Put the required elements of a formal letter in the correct order, from the top to the bottom of the page, by numbering each point.

- ☐ Your address
- ☐ Your name and/or position
- ☐ Subject of the letter or reference
- ☐ Your signature
- ☐ The correct closing phrase (Yours …)
- ☐ The date
- ☐ The name and address of the person you are writing to
- ☐ The salutation (Dear …)

Structure of the letter

The main content of the letter is likely to include:

- an introductory paragraph – this may thank the reader for an earlier letter or introduce you and explain why you are writing
- main paragraph(s) – these will set out the point(s) you want to make. Each point should have its own paragraph
- closing paragraph – you may end by summing up what you have said, proposing next steps, or saying 'I look forward to hearing from you'

Always use formal language, avoiding slang, abbreviations and jargon.

Checking what you have written

Next time you write a formal letter, use this checklist:

- ☐ Have you included all of the required elements (names, addresses, date, salutation and closing elements)?
- ☐ Have you used headed paper if available?
- ☐ Is the reason you are writing clear?
- ☐ Is the tone of writing polite and professional?
- ☐ Have you used appropriate language?
- ☐ Have you explained why you are writing?
- ☐ Does each main point or idea have its own paragraph?
- ☐ Is everything easy to understand?
- ☐ Is it clear what will happen next?
- ☐ Is your spelling, punctuation and grammar correct?